ADVANCE PRAISE FOR
ZOMBIES ATE MY BUSINESS

"*Zombies Ate My Business* is a quick and enjoyable read that imparts a lot of Jamie Gerdsen's experience and wisdom. A valuable tool for anyone trying to build and maintain a thriving, energizing business."

—Hap Klopp, founder and former CEO of The North Face,
author, lecturer, serial entrepreneur

"Zombies are not only in my favorite movies. As Jamie Gerdsen points out in his new book, they are 'living' in your small businesses, where they are often not noticed until it is too late. Jamie's book is filled with advice for Main Street businesses to stay competitive and profitable and not fall victim to the 'living dead!'"

—Barry Moltz, author, speaker, and radio show host

"The businesses of Main Street—stationery stores, plumbers, hair salons, candy and ice cream shops, small manufacturing or service companies that have been located in the same downtown location for more than three generations—are often overlooked when we talk about innovation, creativity, growth, and employee engagement. Jamie Gerdsen is a spokesperson for Main Street and the advice in his new book, *Zombies Ate My Business*, is solid and entertaining."

—Faisal Hoque, founder of Shadoka, author of
Everything Connects and Survive To Thrive

"Ideal for the CEO/Owner of any small business. Zombies will suck the lifeblood from your precious livelihood. Gerdsen's stories show you how to spike these sleepwalkers with practical plans. Too true not to read."

—Bob Vanourek, former CEO of 5 companies, co-author, *Triple Crown Leadership: Building Excellent, Ethical, and Enduring Organizations*

"Do you have employees who walk around the office like zombies, eating up company time and money by not working effectively and efficiently? As Gerdsen so eloquently writes in *Zombies Ate my Business*, the zombies are not the scary part, the scary part is the wasted money and time that comes from the money eating and unproductive employees found in many businesses. I love metaphors and Gerdsen has found a great one! If you want to become a zombie hunter so you can identify, and more importantly, replace the zombies in your workforce with effective, productive, and engaged employees, read *Zombies Ate my Business*, take good notes, and prepare yourself for the hunt!"

—Howard C. Fero, PhD, The Leadership Doc, author of *Lead Me Out to the Ballgame: Stories and Strategies to Develop Major League Leadership*

ZOMBIES
ATE MY
BUSINESS

How to Keep Your Traditional Business
from Becoming One of the Undead

JAMIE GERDSEN

RIVER GROVE
BOOKS

Published by River Grove Books
Austin, Texas
www.rivergrove.com

Distributed by River Grove Books

For ordering information or special discounts for bulk purchases, please contact Greenleaf Book Group at PO Box 91869, Austin, TX 78709, 512.891.6100.

Design and composition by Greenleaf Book Group
Cover design by Greenleaf Book Group
Cover image: ©iStockphoto.com/RUSSELLTATEdotCOM

Cataloging-in-Publication data is available.

Hardcover ISBN: 978-1-63299-070-9

Paperback ISBN: 978-1-63299-060-0

eBook ISBN: 978-1-63299-061-7

First Edition

HERE'S TO THE CRAZY ONES—the misfits, the rebels, the troublemakers, the round pegs in the square holes. The ones who see things differently—they're not fond of rules. You can quote them, disagree with them, glorify or vilify them, but the only thing you can't do is ignore them because they change things. They push the human race forward, and while some may see them as the crazy ones, we see genius, because the ones who are crazy enough to think that they can change the world, are the ones who do.

—Steve Jobs

CONTENTS

I WANT TO THANK my family. Without their unwavering support I never would have believed I could accomplish what I have. To my boys, Jack and Pete, you continually make me a better person every day. To the team members at Apollo, each one of you has made our team better. Your continual belief in our fanatical approach to the customer experience is humbling.

KEEPING AND GETTING CUSTOMERS FOR LIFE BY PROVIDING A FLAWLESS CUSTOMER EXPERIENCE.

I know what it takes to be exceptional:

- *I will deliver a "Wow" customer experience.*
- *I will never stop improving—myself, my work, my knowledge, my example.*

- *I will build strong customer relationships.*
- *I will own the challenges I meet every day.*

I'm a winner!
I'm an Apollo Fanatic!

APOLLO

I SEE . . .

Perhaps you recall the scene in the movie *The Sixth Sense*, when 9-year-old Cole Sear (Haley Joel Osment) tells child psychologist Dr. Malcolm Crowe (Bruce Willis) his secret, in a whispery thin voice: "I see dead people . . . walking around like regular people."

Well, I've been looking over your business and I want to tell you something: "I see zombies . . . walking around like regular employees."

"*Zombies*?" you ask. "Come on, Jamie. Really?"

Yup. And you need to listen, or those zombies will eat up your business.

Gulp. Gulp. Gone.

Read on, and find out just how invasive those zombies have already become and how much they'll go on gulping until they devour your entire business.

Now the zombies I'm talking about don't look like the ones you see on the hit TV show *The Walking Dead* or in the movie *World War Z*. They don't have hideously disfigured faces, blood dripping down on torn shreds of clothing; they don't emit a rotting-corpse smell. If they did, they'd be easy to spot and super easy to eliminate from your business.

Oh, no. These zombies are much more difficult to identify. They're hidden in plain sight, moving around the office or job site, seemingly doing their jobs and responding to other workers. But they're in a decidedly indifferent state. Call it a self-induced hypnosis or even sleepwalking through the business day. Whatever it is, these individuals are not invested in moving your business forward. In fact, they're not interested in your business. Period. They're interested in one thing and one thing only—collecting a paycheck for doing the absolute minimum amount of work. And don't make the mistake of thinking this applies only to the lowly serfs in the trenches. Zombies have been known to walk the management halls, too.

No matter where zombies exist in your organization, their indifference is infectious. They cause other people to disengage. Very quickly, they create a lethargic, indifferent work force. Think of it as the first course in a zombie meal.

What's the next course? you ask. Human flesh? Or perhaps that zombie favorite, human brains?

No, I'm afraid it's much, much worse.

They're going to eat your money.

CHAPTER 2

BECOMING A ZOMBIE HUNTER

Bet you never thought "zombie hunter" would be one of your most important executive tasks. Get used to it; we are living in a strange new world.

The old days, when workers showed up on time and gave everything they had, have now gone the way of Nehru jackets and parachute pants. Having a strong work ethic means different things to different people. For me, a strong work ethic is nothing short of giving a job your all—or as an athlete might say: "leaving it all on the field."

But for too many employees, it means simply showing up for work, socializing over coffee, and then settling in to the important stuff: Facebook, Twitter feeds, YouTube. Whew! I'm ready to go home already.

Yes, I'm being harsh. Everyone wants to work in an office environment where the individual isn't a slave to the job and has plenty of freedom to interact with the world outside the office. I get that. I even agree with it.

But the issue is productivity.

While the new, more enlightened work environment was designed to make employees happier and more productive, it has also become an ideal hiding place for zombies.

They blend in.

That's why your job—as zombie hunter—is to identify them and weed them out. Cull the nonproductive ones from the herd. Each person who isn't being productive is sucking the life out of your business. The more zombies you have, the more dead weight your business is forced to carry.

Most traditional businesses—others, too, for that matter—can't afford to lug around this dead weight. But let's stick with traditional businesses, for a moment, since that's my passion.

I define traditional businesses as mainstay businesses: dry cleaners, auto parts supply stores, gas stations, HVAC companies, plumbers, and electricians. Even some manufacturing facilities fall into the traditional business category.

You know these companies. They live where you live.

It's the plumber two streets over who hung out his shingle in 1953; the dry cleaner down the block that now has second-generation ownership; the manufacturer near the highway exit, that has had a steady work force of fifty-five employees for three decades.

Traditional businesses have stood the test of time, been bastions of the community, and are—in most cases—doing business in the same way they always have. You see, for most traditional businesses, each year is pretty much a repeat of the previous year.

What do I mean by that?

Let's use my business, Apollo, as an example.

The company started in 1910—long before I was even born. For sixty years, it was a single-service company—heating. When air conditioning came on the scene in the 1950s, Apollo added air conditioning installation and service. But since heating and air conditioning go hand in hand, for all intents and purposes, Apollo Heating & Cooling was still a single-service company. The business model didn't change. It was still technicians doing installation and servicing for customers in the same way they always had.

The key word here is "same."

Year in and year out, the employees at Apollo were the *same*: the services we offered were the *same*, the products we installed were the *same*, and we worked for the *same* customers.

With so much sameness, you can see how it's easy to get lulled into a comforting routine. Before you know it, your whole business is, well, kinda zombie-like.

Just like that, you and your company resemble the walking dead. And this can lead to three very bad outcomes:

1. **That comfortable routine of sameness is like heroin.** Suddenly, it's all you want. When this happens, you ignore problems, you Band-Aid problems instead of fixing them. You begin managing the business differently. Instead of making decisions based on who or what needs to be done to grow, you base them on what will cause you the least disruption.

2. **Undead companies are sleepwalkers.** Sure, they're still running service calls. Making products. Hiring and firing. Filing taxes. But make no mistake—they're doing it in a trance. These companies have lost the drive that fosters growth. They're just cruising along. In effect, they've "plateaued," which is deadly dangerous. It doesn't take much to nudge a plateaued business into decline and death.

3. **Undead businesses are zombie magnets.** Zombie employees swarm to them. Why? Pretty simple: they love the sameness. It's a great environment to settle in and do as little as possible. The more zombies your undead business attracts, the more dead weight it has to carry, and the faster it's going to go into decline.

Your job as owner/CEO/CZH (chief zombie hunter) is to prevent your business from joining the ranks of the undead. Throughout this book there are tools that will help you reenergize your business—propelling growth, and making it a zombie-free zone.

It takes smart mojo to make that happen. But I'm going to teach you the secrets.

Exercises:

☑ Zombies are employees who have emotionally disengaged from your business. Because they've disengaged, they're no longer helping your business grow. As you look at your employees, do you see obvious zombies among them?

☑ Do you have zombies in your management ranks? These are often people who like to tell others what to do but seldom do any actual work themselves. Make a list of those who exhibit zombie-like behavior.

☑ Take your list of potential zombies and identify those people you wish to save. Understand that this is an emotional and time-intensive process. Often, management zombies have institutional memory, which makes them extremely valuable to the organization. Bringing those individuals back can often reenergize an organization.

☑ Finally, are you—that's right, *you*—exhibiting any zombie-like behavior? Has it all gotten to be routine? Have you, as CEO/owner, grown too comfortable in that corner office?

+   +   +

As we continue, we'll talk about what you can do to reengage emotionally to make your business grow and become more profitable.

CHAPTER 3

ZOMBIE BITES

Here's one of those "*Oh, crap*" moments.

I wanted to give you instances of how zombies feed on your business, but I didn't want these stories to cause problems for those who might recognize themselves in my examples.

So I'm approaching this the way movies do when they say "based on a true story." The key word is "based." It allows filmmakers to add a 100 mph car chase, blow up three buildings, and have the hero save all the children at a local preschool.

Gotta love the movies.

TECH INFECTION

A traditional business that specialized in carpet cleaning added a new tech. They were pleased with the hire because Dan had worked for another carpet cleaner and brought experience with him. Just to be sure, the company paired him with Jason, one of their more experienced techs, and Jason confirmed Dan knew his stuff.

For the first six months, Dan was a model employee. But then, he seemed to slow down. When supervisors questioned why his jobs always seemed to be running long, he shrugged it off, blaming faulty equipment, health issues, scheduling mix-ups—a whole litany of woes.

But the truth was, Dan—knowing his probationary period was over—was slowing down to his usual speed. If the rest of the techs in the company were working at 60 mph, Dan was doing 35.

He was also telling any techs who'd listen that they didn't need to hustle to finish their jobs. "Why bust your chops for them?" he'd say. "The company has plenty of money and besides, when you take longer, customers feel they're getting more for their money."

Guess what?

Other techs started working slower, too. It was a full quarter later before management realized the effect Dan had had on productivity. If, in round numbers, the company normally grossed $650,000 a quarter, that quarter they grossed $550,000.

Word had gotten out about Dan's zombie-like work speed and he was put on a performance improvement plan (PIP). At the end of the PIP, he was let go. But the damage had been done. The next quarter's gross was better, at $575,000. But the company was now down $75,000 for the year.

Even worse, to get the rest of the techs back operating at normal speed, the company had to put on an incentive—which was an additional expense.

FATAL FINALE

A decade ago, Dave, the CEO of a traditional business with seventy-five employees, changed his company from a sole proprietorship to an employee-owned business. At the time, he told his employees his exit strategy was to sell them the company. More than thirty employees bought shares. Four key VPs purchased sizable stakes, each believing that he or she might become the next CEO.

In fact, each of these VPs continued to buy stock, thinking (well . . . Dave might have intimated) that whoever owned the most stock might have a leg up on becoming CEO.

Dave, however, never put a succession plan in place. He liked the competition in acquiring shares and he knew if he tapped one of them, the other three might leave.

So as he came closer to retirement, he kept dangling the CEO carrot, all the while pulling as much money out of the company as possible. In his final years, he spent much of his time at his fishing cabin in Canada.

The day he retired, he gathered the four VPs together in his office overlooking the shop floor, looked each of them in the eye and said: "I don't know which of you will be best to run the company so I'm going to let you decide that among yourselves."

All four wanted it. None of them were willing to concede. The impasse continued for three weeks, during which time none of the company's employees knew who was running the place and little work was accomplished.

The VPs finally settled it at an off-site slugfest by voting their shares. The VP who owned the most shares teamed with the VP who owned the least—electing themselves, respectively, CEO and president.

One of the VPs quit on the spot. And her shares then had to be repurchased by the company.

The remaining VP stayed and sabotaged anything and everything he could, which was especially hurtful because the company was so weak.

The new CEO quickly discovered his predecessor had stripped the company bare—of a substantial amount of working capital.

Seven months later, after three rounds of layoffs, the company closed its doors.

This happens all too often when the head guy goes zombie and becomes psychotically greedy.

MY SON, THE ZOMBIE

Steve built a thriving service business. Much of the company's success was pure Steve. He was a handsome guy, always ready with a smile and an encouraging word. But he was more than just a nurturing boss; he made smart decisions and viewed running his business as a marathon, not a sprint.

People liked working for Steve. And because they liked him, they were emotionally invested in the company and worked hard. In fact, Steve's company became one of those rare companies where people in his business all wanted to work.

That all changed when Steve Jr. joined the company as EVP—executive vice president.

Steve Jr. had inherited his dad's good looks and charm but not his work ethic. Even in high school he told friends: "I don't have to study, I'm going to inherit my dad's company and I'll be set for life." After Steve Jr. failed out of his third college, his dad brought him into the company and put him in charge of corporate accounts.

It took almost a year before corporate accounts began to atrophy. A loss here. A loss there. Of course, Steve never saw it as Junior's fault. Instead, two years later—with corporate accounts still declining—Dad named him EVP of Sales and Marketing.

For the first time Junior found something he enjoyed—being wined and dined by the company's advertising agency and various media outlets. During an agency marketing presentation, Steve Jr. had an idea.

A wonderful, terrible idea.

An idea that would show his dad how smart he was. And, even better, he wouldn't have to lift a finger.

He'd fire the ad agency, save the company all the money it was paying them, get out of all that costly media, and go into freestanding inserts (commonly known as FSIs). The beauty of FSIs was that they would do the creative work for free; and because they dealt in coupons, they could provide Junior with a black-and-white, quantifiable, provable record of marketing spend and sales.

He enthusiastically pitched it to his dad, who was skeptical, but figured it couldn't hurt the company too much.

So the agency was let go and Steve Jr.—not wanting to get his hands dirty doing the hard work of figuring out a profitable ad campaign—instructed the FSI publisher to think up a really good promotion. (And, of course, to continue wining and dining him.) They presented their idea—a 15 percent discount on a service call—over a filet mignon dinner paired with a vintage red wine. It might have been the wine talking, but Junior thought it was the best idea he'd ever heard. He didn't even bother running it past his dad.

An FSI with 15 percent off coupon was created and ran in the FSI pubs. Redemption was almost immediate. People started using those coupons.

Junior was thrilled.

But the CFO was livid.

That 15 percent discount took out most of the company's profit. Worse, before they could get out of all their FSI contracts, they were actually training consumers not to use their service unless they got a discount.

The company took a 9 percent hit in their profits that first year. Without the exposure of mass-media marketing, the company's profits declined 21 percent in year two.

Most employees who'd thought Steve Jr. was just lazy now realized that was not the case.

He was lazy *and* not very smart.

Of course his dad had no choice but to stick up for him. This, in turn, began to polarize the company.

Today, Steve Jr. is still EVP, but he has no real authority. And hey, that's fine by him. Zombies love a fat paycheck for just sitting around and looking important.

ZOMBIE DAYS OFF

A traditional business hired a young woman, Meagan, as a dispatcher. She was personable, had good references, and seemed to have a knack for juggling service teams. For this traditionally male company, Meagan was something different—a walk on the wild side.

She had been with the company for just over two years when she took her first sick day. It was a Friday. She called in that morning and said she was too sick to come in. And then on Monday, just three days later, she showed up looking fit as a fiddle.

Friday rolled around and she called in sick again. Monday she was fine.

She missed four Fridays in a row before her supervisor called her into his office and nicely asked her what was going on.

Meagan broke down in tears and said she was seeing a psychiatrist on Fridays because of workplace issues.

The supervisor was stunned. Workplace issues? Psychiatrist? He tried to get her to tell him more, but all he got was a torrent of tears. A little worried about a lawsuit, he told her about a resource that could help her manage the situation and even helped set up times for her to meet with professionals trained to sort out concerns such as Meagan's. He then worked with the staff to identify how they could improve the work environment, and he followed through on their suggestions. Even Meagan told him she was pleased with the changes.

But she continued her Friday absences. She was now essentially working four days a week but being paid for five.

The supervisor's boss got involved. This four days' work for five days' pay had him infuriated.

The three met, and the supervisor's boss told Meagan she needed to either start working five days a week like everyone else or risk termination.

Meagan began crying and between sobs informed the two men that she was thinking of filing a gender discrimination lawsuit because what she'd endured at the company (never elaborating on exactly what) had ruined her health; even though the company had spent time and resources addressing her concerns; and even though she, herself, had told the supervisor the atmosphere had greatly improved.

Now the supervisor's boss was stunned. A lawsuit? He didn't want that. To ward off any possible legal action he suggested Meagan take a three-month leave of absence *with* pay so she could, as he put it, *get healthy*.

Of course, zombies like Meagan never get healthy. They just burrow in deeper and deeper, costing the company more and more money.

PEST CONTROL CAN'T CONTROL ZOMBIES

Burt never wanted to work at the pest control company his grandfather founded and his father ran. To get away, he joined the military and traveled halfway around the world, doing two tours in Iraq, before returning home to go to college.

During the first semester of Burt's junior year, two weeks before Thanksgiving, his mom called to tell him his father had suffered a stroke while getting ready for work. His father died on the way to the hospital.

Burt went home for the funeral, fully expecting to return to school. That wasn't to be. His mom needed him to run the business.

Because Burt hadn't had any interest in the business, he wasn't sure what to expect. His first day, sitting in his father's chair at his father's desk, he didn't think he was up to it. But the staff, still shocked by his father's death, rallied around him.

Burt dug in and did an inventory of company assets. On the

positive side of the ledger—he placed the staff. On the negative side of the ledger—he placed pretty much everything else.

Their building was old and cramped. The fleet desperately needed replacing. The computer system was generations behind. The office joke was that they were still using equipment Burt's grandfather had purchased.

The company was heavily in debt—they'd maxed out their line of credit with the bank and hadn't made a principal payment in over a year.

Burt thought seriously about shutting the doors. But the never-give-up training he'd gotten in the military made him determined to turn the business around.

He knew this wasn't a task he could handle by himself, so he reached out to SCORE (the volunteer nonprofit association supported by the US Small Business Association) and put together a plan to reinvigorate the business.

As part of the plan, Burt took no salary for that first year and reinvested everything back into the business. He worked hundred-hour weeks doing anything that would help the business get out of the hole.

Friday afternoon, on one of those hundred-hour weeks, one of his techs, Wayne, stopped by his office. Wayne wanted an increase in his hourly wage. Burt explained that the company wasn't in a position to do that right now, but if Wayne could bring in more business, Burt would see about giving him a bump at some point in the future.

Wayne, however, wasn't interested in working to get the company more business. He decided if the company wouldn't give him what he deserved, then he'd just have to moonlight—in broad daylight.

Using the company's truck, equipment, and chemicals, he started working (mostly on company time) for himself. Instead of billing the customer with company invoices, he pocketed the cash. So in essence he was running a business for himself inside the business. He got away with it for nine months, before Burt figured out Wayne was using considerably more chemicals than the other techs. Small wonder. At his peak, Wayne had thirty-eight customers he was servicing with the company's equipment but who were paying him directly.

When Burt confronted him, Wayne told him, "It was all your fault. You should've given me that raise I wanted when I asked for it."

Zombies have no shame.

+   +   +

What's the common thread in these four stories? Pretty obvious. Especially in this last story. Zombies are only in it for themselves. They could not care less about your business. If the business folds, they'll just move on and create havoc at the next place.

The sad thing is you're paying them to do this to you. The costs to you—in terms of salary, negative impact on other employees, lost income, and theft—are outrageous.

The only comparison I can offer is shoplifting. This is a huge problem for retail stores that have thousands of dollars walk out of their stores annually. Bad as that is, what a zombie can do to you is far worse.

Lest you think I see zombies in every business, let me share one more story.

ZOMBIE-FREE ZONE

I bought my lawnmower at a family-owned John Deere dealership. The place is amazing. When I take my mower in for its yearly tune-up, there's always someone ready to help me. They get the mower back to me promptly. They charge fairly. And get this: they're helpful. Actually helpful. Let me just say it again for emphasis—helpful. What I mean by helpful is that they are proactive to my needs. It is almost like they know what I want before I do. This almost always ensures that they will get more share of wallet with each customer.

The fourth generation of family members is now working in the business. But family members aren't treated any differently than nonfamily members, and everybody there—family or non-family—works hard.

Like genuinely good people, there are genuinely good businesses. I think that starts when a person of character sets the tone and establishes a caring, considerate company culture. That's what happened here. Succeeding generations have only strengthened that culture.

Zombies know this isn't a place for them. So they keep moving right down the street.

Exercises:

☑ Have you had instances where you were victimized by a zombie? If so, in retrospect, what could you have done to limit the damage?

☑ Having heard these examples, do you see that you have zombies in your organization now? How much damage are they causing? Put together a game plan for dealing with them.

☑ Do you know a business with a strong positive culture—like my John Deere dealership? How could you strengthen your culture? Strengthening the culture is measured, in my mind, by something interesting the CEO of a large company once asked me. He said, "How fast do your associates drive to work, compared to how fast they drive away?"

CHAPTER 4

THE BUSINESS LIFE CYCLE

One of the reasons zombies are so harmful to traditional businesses is that most traditional businesses fall into the mature or declining segments of the business life cycle. Zombies in those segments can quickly destroy the health of a business and start a fast slide to death.

Now you may be thinking, *I didn't know a business had a life cycle*. Well, they do. One that's very similar to our own (see Figure 4.1).

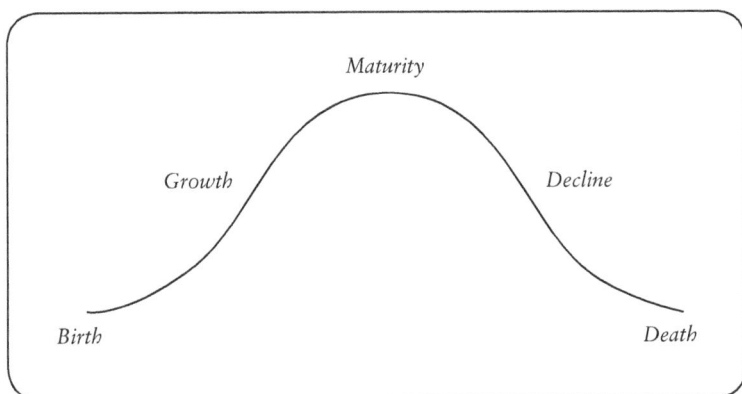

Figure 4.1 The Business Life Cycle

Companies are born. They grow up. They mature. They decline. And, unfortunately, they die.

Let's take a closer look at each of the life-cycle stages and the attributes of each.

BIRTH

New companies are born all the time. Tech start-ups seem to be the ones that get all the attention. Largely unnoticed, however, in communities across the nation, traditional businesses are constantly sprouting up. What do they look like?

It could be a tech who worked for a heating and cooling or electrical company who decides to go out on his own.

It could be an entrepreneur opening her own storefront.

It could be a manufacturer making product in his garage.

For all of these businesspeople, the excitement of starting that business is palpable. You feel that adrenalin rush. Your heart beats faster. You're giddy with your prospects for the future.

This is a time where everybody pulls together. It's a crusade, a mission, a calling. It's late nights and cold pizza. It's being on the high wire with no safety net—it's just you, your energy, your imagination, and your drive.

Problems? Obstacles? This is a time where people leap tall buildings in a single bound.

Boy, is it a heady atmosphere. No wonder the lucky souls who get to experience a start-up remember it as the most exciting time of their business careers.

You're creating something that didn't exist before—a business with your DNA. That's right, your DNA. Yours.

Wow.

GROWTH

All that enthusiasm generated in the birth phase fuels growth. Many times, that starts with word of mouth. People talk up the new company. This is the original viral marketing. A job done well for one customer causes that customer to tell friends, generating more jobs. And those jobs generate still more jobs.

Before you know it, your dance card is full.

Early growth is very validating. That insecurity you felt about starting a business? It melts away. You gain new confidence that your business is sustainable.

That early glow of gratitude fades slowly but surely. After a few years of growth, it becomes *expected*. You heard right, *expected*. Without realizing it, you've begun to take growth for granted.

Many companies at this stage believe growth will continue forever. Just keep doing what you're doing and growth will continue. Oh, if it were only that simple. While growth may very well continue for years, the decisions you make—or don't make—early in the growth curve may determine how long that growth lasts. See Figure 4.2 to see what I'm talking about.

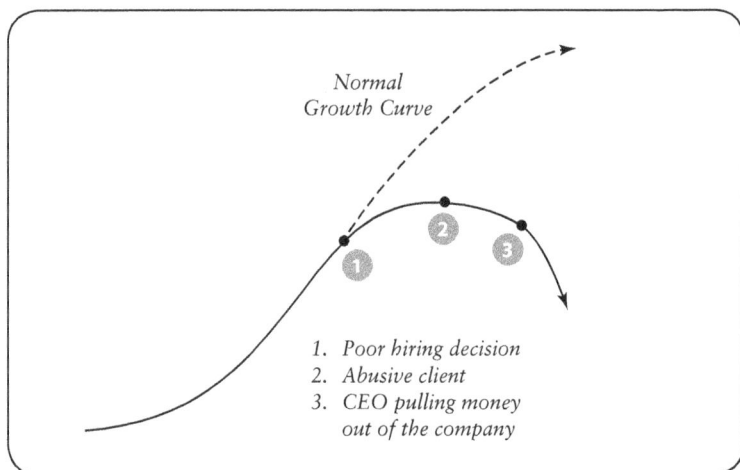

Figure 4.2 *Poor Decisions Flatten the Growth Curve and Lead to Early Decline*

For example, a bad key hire can be a real momentum killer. If that person—for whatever reason—isn't a good fit, coming to grips with that will cause the company to spend precious energy on internal matters rather than on external customer relations.

Second example: Take on a bad client and that client can demoralize your staff. An abusive client will make everyone's day less pleasant. And no matter how much money they're paying you, that abuse takes a toll. Before you know it, you, and everyone who works with you, will dread coming into the office.

Third example: if you, as the CEO/owner, decide the business is your personal piggy bank and start pulling money out as fast as you can, you're diverting resources that should be fueling future growth. Every time I see a Lamborghini parked in a space marked CEO, I think *he's driving the company's future.*

Fourth example (and the most insidious and dangerous one): **You get in a rhythm, the rhythm becomes a routine, and the routine becomes a religion.** The religion becomes your mantra about how you do business and you're loath to change it. In fact, you become so enamored with it that you couldn't change it if you wanted to. The ruts become too deep to steer the company away from oncoming dangers. When you hear the expression "adapt or die," well, these are the companies that would rather die.

The growth phase should be a time to develop a management structure and institutionalize best practices. By using growth to build a strong, sustainable company culture, you're paying that growth forward.

A forward-thinking company will find ways to always stay in the growth phase.

MATURITY

No matter how strong a company's growth has been or how long it has lasted, if the company stays strictly with its core offering, that growth will begin to diminish. This slipping into maturity isn't something that's noticeable. You don't go to work one day, look around, and say, "Hmmm. This is now a mature company."

Maturity—that flattening of the growth curve—sneaks up on you. And it can happen for a whole host of different reasons.

Market Competition

New competition can enter the marketplace. As supply exceeds demand, growth will slow. This is a situation we see continually in the heating and cooling business. The HVAC marketplace is already overpopulated, but new HVAC companies still try to give it a go. They last for a short time, cause angst, fits, and flare-ups at the established HVAC companies, and then disappear.

Financial Health

A company's finances may send it into early maturity. In this case, the company has taken on too much debt. Management may be butting its head against the top of the credit line and doesn't have enough operating capital to keep on growing. You know the old saw: *It takes money to make money.* Well, let's look at it in the context of fueling growth: *If you have less money, you make less money.*

Internal Politics

Internal politics inevitably turn nasty. There are so many ways this can happen, it's positively scary. It could be the department heads for service and installation vying for a promotion. It could be nonfamily members resentful of family members. It could be the older generation versus the younger generation. Whatever it is, it's a real damper on growth. Stamp it out as soon as you see it pop up.

Happy at a Certain Size

The company's CEO may think the company is as big as he or she wants it to be. I've met CEOs who like to micromanage and want to keep the company at a size that allows them to control every tiny detail.

Needy Client

A company's needy client—or worse, clients—may stunt growth, too. In this case, a large client who demands constant attention can severely limit the amount of time the company has for other clients. In some cases, you might grow as the needy client grows, but many times the client doesn't grow and keeps you from growing.

Size of the Bowl

My favorite is the goldfish-bowl effect. To understand this, you have to know that goldfish (real live fish, I'm talking about here) grow only to the size of their fishbowl. Small bowl, and the fish will stay small. Bigger bowl, and they'll grow bigger. The same is true for companies. Their size is often determined by the size of their facilities.

I knew a window manufacturer who had demand for—round numbers—seven thousand windows a year. His manufacturing facility could produce only five thousand windows in a given year. Because he didn't want to enlarge his facility, outsource, or add a third shift, his facility determined his maximum sales. Which was too bad, because he left a lot of market demand on the table.

A friend of mine had his plumbing business in a converted two-story house on the outskirts of the neighborhood business district. He had parking in the back for four trucks. He often said he wished he could add another plumber, but he never did. He didn't have room for the truck.

✦   ✦   ✦

Here's the important takeaway about maturity. As the growth line levels out, it can take one of three paths (see Figure 4.3):

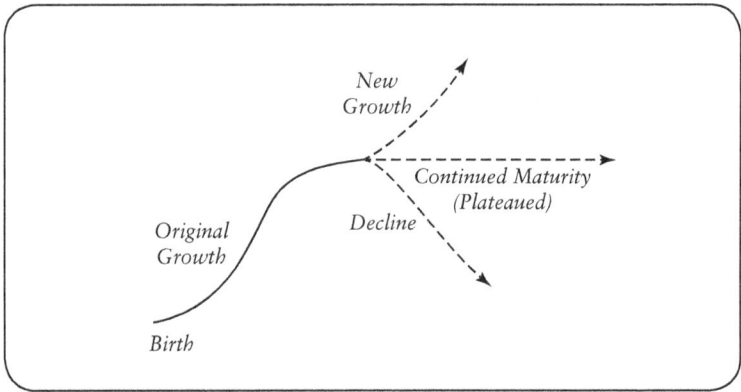

Figure 4.3 The Three Paths

- **It can go up on a continuing basis.** The company is shifting back into growth mode.

- **It can stay level.** In this case the company has plateaued. Of course, nothing stays perfectly level. There will be small increases and small declines.

- **It can head down on a continuing basis.** This is decline. Depending on the rate of decline, the company may not be able to recover.

DECLINE

Watching companies in decline is painful. As an outsider, you see some of the problems and you want to tell them to do this or that to get them back on track. But the truth of the matter is that companies in decline are seldom in a position to make corrections to save themselves.

Let's revisit some of the factors we discussed in the maturity phase and see what happens in decline.

Market Competition

New competitors enter the market and you lose market share. This strengthens them and weakens you. To combat these new competitors, you may have to significantly increase marketing or cut prices. This is often difficult to do when revenues are declining.

Financial Health

A financially sick company is a lot like a sick human. You may need to see a doctor (consultant or bank officer), go on a restricted diet (trim staff, limit spending), exercise more (increase customer outreach), and take your medicine (you, as the CEO/owner, may need to cut back your income from the company).

Doing any or all of this at a time when the company is weakened is tough.

Internal Politics

As a company declines, there are even more things to fight about. Fingers will definitely be pointed as to who is at fault for the decline. The bickerers will all adamantly believe they own the solution but have nothing to do with the problems. The steeper the decline, the louder and more divisive the arguing.

Happy at a Certain Size

Decline will cause a CEO who micromanages to get even deeper into the weeds. He's virtually going to disappear in the tall grass, never realizing that his need to make every decision is the actual root of the problem.

Needy Client

A needy client, sensing decline, is like a shark in the water. It smells blood, and whips itself into a feeding frenzy demanding more, more, more.

Size of the Bowl

This is an odd one. Companies who have derived their size from their bowl are reluctant to take action. They've turned down possible growth because of the physical limitations, and now that they're in decline, they'll be indifferent to that, too.

+   +   +

Remember, decline starts slowly. The drop accelerates as decline builds up speed. If you're going to turn it around, your chances are far better at the beginning of the cycle. At the end, it's like a freight train roaring at full speed toward . . .

DEATH

So everybody comes to work one day and finds the doors locked. Ouch. Maybe there's a note taped to the door saying CLOSED. Maybe not.

The shock for the employees gathered outside on the sidewalk is overwhelming. Shock quickly turns to anger. How could this happen? What am I going to do? I have a family to feed. Bills to pay. What can be done to get the doors open again?

The sad answer is: nothing. Death is unsettling, messy, and worst of all, final.

Exercises:

☑ Chart your business on the business life cycle. Where are you now? Growth? Maturity? Decline? What are key events that may have shifted you from one phase to the next?

☑ Having charted your business, if you are currently in the growth, maturity, or decline phase, what actions can you take to keep your business from moving into the next phase?

CHAPTER 5

THE PERSONAL LIFE CYCLE

In 2004, when I bought Apollo from my dad, the business was, as he described it, cresting. That's putting it mildly. On the business life cycle, Apollo was a plateaued mature business, trending slightly toward decline.

In my earlier book, *Squirrels, Boats, and Thoroughbreds*, I chronicled many of Apollo's issues: poor operating systems, undisciplined employees, supervisors dogging it. You get the gist.

That's no knock on my dad.

He'd been a good shepherd of the business. But at 60-plus years of age, the personal life cycle was catching up with him. He'd survived bad partners, a thieving CFO, downturns in the economy, and waves of outside competition.

I always thought he handled all that with grace and a smile. What I never saw was how alone he'd become and how the responsibility of the business weighed on him.

I mention this because **where you are on the personal life cycle greatly influences events in the business life cycle.**

So what's the personal life cycle?

No great mystery here, it's pretty much the phases you'd expect. However, we're going to identify these phases as time periods. See Figure 5.1.

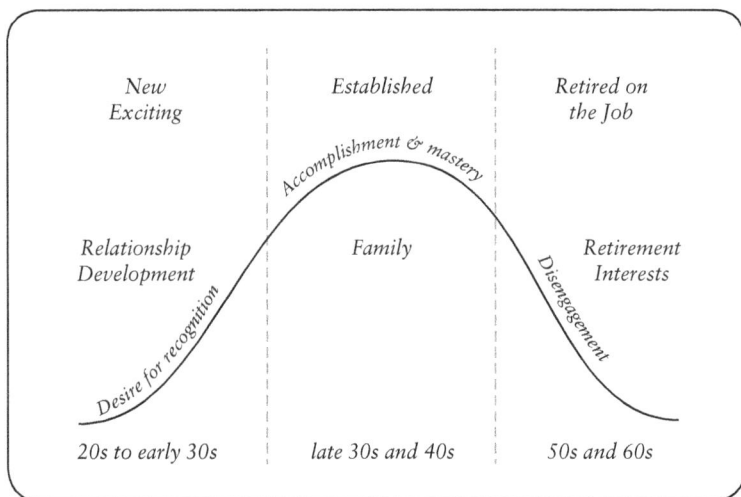

Figure 5.1 The Personal Life Cycle

20s TO EARLY 30s

In your 20s, you're looking to establish yourself. This is the time when new entrants to the workplace want to make their bones. Everything is new; everything is exciting. You're meeting new people, networking. Building your resume. And the thing you want most is the opportunity to show people what you can do.

Given that opportunity, workers in this age group will practically knock down walls to make things happen.

Through a business association, I got to know a young man

in his late 20s who was given the opportunity to head the company's electrical division. The fellow was an avid softball player who was on two summer league teams. When he received the promotion, he dropped softball completely and devoted himself to the job—seventy-hour weeks were the norm. He went at it that way for over a year, dropping 25 pounds in the process. But he tripled sales. That got him the recognition he craved and a second promotion.

A 23-year-old I met recently really impressed me. Just out of college, she couldn't find a job doing what she wanted. Instead of feeling sorry for herself, she identified the top three companies for which she'd like to work. Then she made them an offer they couldn't refuse—she'd work free for one year just to get her foot in the door.

Pretty gutsy.

One of them took her up on it. She worked days for them—free. She took an evening job to earn enough to live on. Or almost live on. She was slowly going broke. Fortunately, after five months, her day job company was so impressed they made her a paid employee.

Just goes to show the resourcefulness and resilience young people have. If you, as a businessperson, need to energize your business, hire a bunch of 20- or 30-year olds. Their energy is exhilarating.

LATE 30s AND 40s

As the 20- and 30-year-olds gain some of that recognition they crave, they begin to settle in. Part of this settling in is business, part is personal.

These late 30s and 40-year-olds now have ten or more years of experience on the job. It's not new to them anymore. Work is now a known commodity. They've gained experience, established themselves, and have moved on from entry-level jobs to senior or management positions.

As their work life is becoming more routine, their personal life is becoming more demanding. Spouses, children, ex-spouses, stepchildren, and aging parents all require time and attention.

I knew a young go-getter who worked sixty- to eighty-hour weeks to be the highest achiever in his company. He pretty much lived at the office. He reveled in how many jobs he handled and disdained others who didn't put in as many hours or work as hard. His hard work was noticed and he was rewarded.

But life changed for him after he married. The sixty- to eighty-hour weeks were replaced by fifty-hour weeks. He still worked as hard, just not as long. Then children happened. One child. Two. Three. Before he knew it, he was running kids to school, coaching a kid's soccer team, and carting his crew to activities. His workweek took a hit. Many weeks, it was below forty hours. Some weeks, it was seriously below forty. And with all the family interruptions, his time at the office wasn't nearly as productive.

The dedicated company man aged into the dedicated family man. I applaud him. He's a great husband and dad. His company, however, lost a driver. You can almost see the business's curve flattening.

Health is the other issue people in this age bracket must contend with. People think they're invincible in their 20s. It's a different story in those late 30s and 40s. They're a pain. Literally.

I knew a carpenter who built a business doing whole-house remodeling. He had subs for the HVAC, plumbing, and electric work, but he did all the tear-out, carpentry, drywall, and finish work himself. He did high-quality work and consequently had great buzz.

He was also a foodie who loved a good meal. His weight rose in his 30s and 40s and by the time he hit 50, that spare tire around his middle would have fit an 18-wheeler. All that weight caused knee pain. While he was dealing with that, he hurt his back pulling out a Jacuzzi during a bathroom remodel.

He continued to work. But he was never the same and neither was the business. Health caused his business's growth curve to flatten.

Whatever the reason, during their mid-30s and 40s, most employees slow down, settle into a groove, and stay there. They can be extremely productive, but they no longer view work as an exciting new adventure.

They view work as, well, work.

50s AND 60s

I once heard an HR person dismissing older workers, saying those in their 50s were in preretirement mode and those in their 60s were in full-retirement mode. That may be a little exaggerated in an economic environment where people often need to work into their 70s to retire, but it rings true about many employees.

I've observed people in their 60s who have all but retired on the job. Here's how that happens: they're still working, but mentally they've checked out. Similarly, I've seen employees in their 50s who were halfway checked out, putting in whatever effort it took to keep from making their meager efforts obvious.

We had a manager who'd given twenty-four years of service. He wore each of those years like a badge. And for collecting all those badges, the only work he thought he needed to do was to tell others what to do. To be honest, he didn't even want to do that. He wanted to stay in his office and not have anyone bother him. Of course, after twenty-four years, he was at the top of his pay grade. So he was collecting a pretty good salary for maintaining heat on a seat.

I knew another 60-something whose kids were finally out of the house. She was a dispatcher, good at running crews, but she and her husband (who was older and already retired) wanted to travel, so she began using all her vacation, all her sick days, and as much unpaid time off as she could get. Her absences kept operations in a constant state of flux. When her boss told her, "No more unpaid time off, we need you here," she took it as a slap in the face and was resentful until the day she retired, when she stormed out, slamming the door behind her.

Not all 60-somethings are that way. To be fair, I've also seen employees in their 60s who'd rather work forever than retire. For them, retirement means being put out to pasture. And they hate the idea.

In general, though, this is a time when employees *are* disengaging, preparing for their lives after they leave the work force. With the horizon line approaching, they want to shed, not take on, responsibility.

✦   ✦   ✦

Got all that? Good. Let's get back to Apollo and my dad. Apollo, you'll remember, we described as a mature business. There was no growth curve. Things were as flat as two-day-old soda. My dad was in his 60s, beginning to disengage. Recipe for disaster? Bet the ranch on it.

That's when I arrived.

I was in my early 30s when I rejoined the company. All piss and vinegar. I started as a commissioned salesman—no salary, strictly commission.

Growing up, you learn a lot about a family business at the dinner table. But no matter how much you've soaked up, there's no substitute for experiencing it firsthand. So when I rejoined, I learned the business bottom to top, saw all its strengths and weaknesses. When the time came, I bought the business from my dad.

I'm not sure everyone who worked at Apollo thought that was a good thing. One long-time employee expressed what many were probably thinking: "With him at the helm, we'll be out of business in no time."

Thankfully, I've proven her wrong.

Here's what she wasn't seeing: Dad, after many years of running the business, had fallen victim to sameness. Because of that, the business was coasting. And frankly, would have started into decline. Apollo was the down escalator and Dad was riding it.

Fortunately, I'm riding the up escalator and, at the convergence of the two, the company changes hands. It now rides up with me, propelled by all that 30-something drive and determination.

I'd like to tell you that kicking a traditional company back into growth mode is that easy, but then I'd be the worst liar since Joe Isuzu. It's tough, but doable. I know because we've done it at Apollo.

For you, it's going to be less difficult. Because I'm going to share insights that will save you time, money, and mistakes.

Exercises:

☑ Where are you—as CEO/owner of a traditional business—in the personal life cycle? How about your key people in the company?

☑ If you fall in the 50s/60s age category, what can you do to energize yourself and your company?

☑ How would adding younger, more growth-oriented employees impact your business? Are there key areas where enthusiasm and drive would lift the entire organization?

CHAPTER 6

MIXING THE TWO TOGETHER

We've just talked about the two life cycles—business and personal. Now it's time to put the two together and see how they interact. Understanding these interactions gives us insight into how to manage both the personal and business sides of the equation. Of course, while an employee's age is obvious and provable (the employer can find date of birth on the job application), it's not as easy for an employee to gauge just what stage of the business life cycle a company is in. That's why it's important for a job seeker to do a bit of digging/do some homework on this aspect of a traditional company before he or she heads to the company's HR with resume in hand.

Here's the matchup by the business's life-cycle stage and employee ages from early 20s to retirement.

BUSINESS STAGE: BIRTH + EMPLOYEE AGE: 20s TO EARLY 30s

Roles: Entrepreneur, Inventor, Anarchist, Visionary

Many consider this nirvana: a *new* company started by *young* people. Yep, we're talking start-ups. Right now, they're the darlings of the business world, and with good reason: They enjoy the best of the two life cycles.

On the personal side, people involved in a start-up are at the point in their lives where they are able to devote large amounts of time and energy. Because they are early in their careers, they view each task, each problem as a challenge and an opportunity. For many of these young entrepreneurs, they aren't engaged so much in business as they are in a quest. They bring to this quest an almost religious fervor that's contagious.

On the business side, everything is new—employees, products, operations, customers. Since the company started as a blank slate, it's easy to see progress in each of these categories, and that progress, that sense of *I built this* is exhilarating. Start-ups often start out in office space that's less than ideal. (How many times have you heard about a multimillion-dollar business that started in a garage?) Office attire might be jeans and t-shirts. The space and the dress code really don't matter in a start-up. All that's important is the quest. And who doesn't want to be part of that excitement? Who doesn't want to be part of a quest?

BUSINESS STAGE: GROWTH + EMPLOYEE AGE: 20s TO EARLY 30s

Roles: Associate, Foot Soldier

A company in its growth phase is looking for hands to handle and extend that growth. The company hires enthusiastic young people, often more than they need, keeping the good ones and discarding the rest, letting their energy propel growth. Because the company's growing, it has the ability to reward star performers, locking in critical talent.

Employees benefit, too. A growth company gives employees the opportunity to make names for themselves, without the risk of starting businesses on their own. Often employees are mentored and can gain knowledge and skills more quickly than they could on their own. Salaries are usually good and, because the company is growing, there's normally largesse with benefits. From a resume standpoint, having worked at a growing company scores points with future employers, particularly if that company enjoys status in its field.

BUSINESS STAGE: MATURITY + EMPLOYEE AGE: 20s TO EARLY 30s

Role: Chum (as in fishing bait)

Mature companies view young employees differently than newer businesses do. Because mature companies have become regimented and operate in a set routine, they're no longer looking for employees to drive growth; they see young employees as cheap and disposable.

That may sound harsh. But a mature company is looking for cheaper replacement parts. If the company can replace a higher-paid employee with a less expensive, younger employee, it's in the mature company's best interests to do so. Forget training. Forget advancement. In a mature company, the young person is there to be used and abused.

For the young employees, it's hard to see why they would be attracted to a mature company—other than being desperate for jobs. Again, because the company is extremely regimented in its operation, these young employees are going to be stuck in repetitive jobs. If they express dissatisfaction, they'll be replaced by other young employees.

BUSINESS STAGE: DECLINE + EMPLOYEE AGE: 20s TO EARLY 30s

Roles: VP of this, VP of that, EVP of Something Else (Titles don't cost anything, especially when the real role here is plugging the dike)

The declining company is desperate and will hire young employees to fill the void caused by the departure of more experienced employees. These new hirings have little to do with the talents of the young employees; they are simply an effort to buy time. For these new hires, it's a disheartening work environment, because current staffers will be more occupied with finding new jobs than they are with their current work. Constant departures and financial pressures make it hard to accomplish anything. Creditors will be calling; clients will be leaving or demanding extra value to stay.

Walk into the workplace of a declining company and you can smell the desperation. It's not pretty, not pretty at all.

For the employee, there is only a sliver of upside, since salaries will be low, benefits may go *poof*, and employees may have to work without the help of outside resources.

That sliver of upside? There is the opportunity for a young employee with exceptional insight to pluck the company's chestnuts out of the fire—although this feat is seldom recognized by the company. The only benefit to the employee is the ability to showcase the feat to future employers.

For a 20- or 30-something, the declining company is like working on a fault line. You feel the vibrations, the shakes, and then without warning, boom, you're on the street. They can't afford you anymore.

BUSINESS STAGE: DEATH + EMPLOYEE AGE: 20s TO EARLY 30s

Roles: Mourner, Scavenger

Little is left on the carcass of a dead company. Most go into the ground leaving behind mountains of debt. The alert young employee might be able to walk away with contacts, newly fulfilled business, or an account that might give a start to a new business. But that's the exception. Usually, the lawyers get the last scraps from the carcass.

+   +   +

Now let's move on to employees in their late 30s and 40s and how they relate to each business stage.

BUSINESS STAGE: BIRTH + EMPLOYEE AGE: LATE 30s AND 40s

Roles: Expert, Authority, Sage

There are two scenarios for 30- and 40-year-olds working in a birth phase company.

The first is that they worked somewhere—possibly a large company—and left to start their own business. This will be a more disciplined start-up than that of the 20- and 30-year-olds, because workers in the late 30s and early 40s range have learned business skills and will approach the start-up in a more financially responsible way. Think of it as a trade-off—a little less out-of-the-box craziness for a smoother, more professional operation.

The second way late 30- and 40-year-olds might work in a new company is through recruitment. If the founders (think inexperienced 20-year-olds) discover they need experience or knowledge in a specific area in order to continue their quest, they have no qualms about going out and hiring the best and the brightest. Hand that task to a headhunter. The lure of stock options can be hard to resist.

Either way, a young company will benefit from the efforts of this age group. They still have energy and drive and, whether they started the company or were recruited to join, they still are determined to make a name for themselves.

BUSINESS STAGE: GROWTH + EMPLOYEE AGE: LATE 30s AND 40s

Roles: Self-Starters, Gladiators, Intrepreneurs[1]

Growth companies like to hire 30- and 40-year olds with training and experience from leaders in their particular field. Growth companies perceive that they are too busy growing and that it's too expensive to hire and train employees without experience. They believe an employee trained elsewhere can jump on the moving train. If that's the case, it's a win/win for the company: The company doesn't have to pay the cost of training, but it capitalizes on what these employees know and leverages it to other employees in the firm.

This can work well for the employee, too. He or she gets immediate responsibility but may also get (because of that training) immediate authority. That's the magic word—authority. With authority, *you* can make things happen, *you* can take the credit, and *you* can be a rising star in the organization.

There's an employee downside, though. Growth companies often develop silos, and within these silos stratification quickly develops. The top people within each silo can be intent only on their own area and can often be at odds with other silos. Top people in each silo often compete to see who's able to make it to an overall corporate position. When this competition happens, there are a few winners and a lot of casualties. Being a casualty throws you into the loser's bracket. Ouch, dude.

---

1 Intrepreneurs are people who take an existing company and grow it, as opposed to entrepreneurs, who start something.

BUSINESS STAGE: MATURITY + EMPLOYEE AGE: LATE 30s AND 40s

Roles: Staff, Associate, Clone

Not surprisingly, mature companies like the proven track record and experience of potential employees in this age group. The mature company wants individuals who settle easily into the company routine, don't make waves, and perpetuate the status quo. Often individuals in this age group are hired to lessen the workload of long-time established workers, who are then able to sit back and enjoy semi-retirement.

These late 30- and 40-year-olds work diligently, thinking that they'll get those jobs when the current crew retires. Some on-the-job training (OJT) and mentoring happens, but for the most part these new employees do the work and the older employees take the kudos.

BUSINESS STAGE: DECLINE + EMPLOYEE AGE: LATE 30s AND 40s

Roles: Rescuer, Lifesaver, Mercenary

In decline, companies use late 30s and 40-year-olds as lifelines. Many times they're hired for their business connections or to impress a potential client. Remember, declining companies are desperate, so they'll promise these individuals the moon. *(Want to be EVP? Want $100,000 or more a year? Want stock options?)* If business actually arrives as a result of that individual's efforts, many or all of those promises will fall by the wayside. The company needs and wants all the income for itself.

Declining companies are constantly shedding people. "Filler" people are often needed to keep current clients happy. This churn can create opportunities for individuals who aren't bothered by the unstable environment, use the time to build personal networks, have the ability to establish relationships on the client side, or are able to showcase unique approaches or talents.

BUSINESS STAGE: DEATH + EMPLOYEE AGE: LATE 30s AND 40s

Role: Job Applicant

The late 30- or 40-year-old saw the handwriting on the wall. The only unknown was when the company would officially kick the bucket.

During the employee's brief tenure, he or she should have used the time to find that next job.

+   +   +

Now let's move on to employees in their 50s and 60s and how they relate to each business stage.

BUSINESS STAGE: BIRTH + EMPLOYEE AGE: 50s AND 60s

Roles: Chairman, Senior Advisor, Figurehead, Graybeard

Nothing creates an air of stability or smooths client nervousness like silver hair. So young companies often hire a 50- or 60-year-old as the company's chairman (or some other highfalutin title) to give the impression the whole place isn't run by a bunch of kids.

Within the company, this person might be the only one in that 50s to 60s age bracket. The employee may have trouble working with a generation that has different values. Sometimes this can be a very lonely gig.

These senior officers add greater or lesser value, depending on the type of company. In a traditional business—say, a new HVAC company—the senior employee may have experience and knowledge that will genuinely guide the company. In this case, the older employee is reassuring to customers, adding real value, and possibly even directing day-to-day operations. Conversely, if the young company is offering new technology—let's say a revolutionary computer app that constantly keeps your HVAC system at optimum mode—the senior employee may be too set in old ways to embrace the new technology and may only add marginal value.

Like winter/spring marriages, some of these relationships endure, while others end acrimoniously.

BUSINESS STAGE: GROWTH + EMPLOYEE AGE: 50s AND 60s

Roles: Star Performer, Supervisor, Mentor

Like young companies, growth companies hire this age group for their experience and knowledge. Growth companies, however, want this expertise to fuel growth. This is often a good fit for both parties because the company gets workers who add to its arsenal of talents. In most cases, the company sees these individuals as "doers" who can make results happen with very little oversight. These employees are often brought in at a supervisory or senior level and can further impact the company by smart management or mentoring of their direct reports.

For 50- and 60-year-olds, this is often a second chance or a final opportunity. The 50-year-old has fifteen years in which to improve his or her position and earning power. The 60-year-old has the opportunity to make a statement that will be the capstone of his or her career. For both, the growth company is the ideal environment because it has the resources to allow older workers to be successful and finish strong.

BUSINESS STAGE: MATURITY + EMPLOYEE AGE: 50s AND 60s

Roles: Semi-Retiree, Office Occupier, Not-My-Jobber

Mature companies will often add 50- and 60-year-olds to flesh out their senior ranks. This is less about performance, and more about keeping things calm and predictable.

At this age, these individuals know how to fit in, what to do, and what not to do. They're noncontroversial hires for the company that wants zero, zip, nada controversy.

Interestingly, many employees at this age are looking for a job where they don't have to work too hard. This would be a problem almost anywhere but at a mature business, where not working too hard is the norm.

This is why so many 50- and 60-year-olds gravitate to mature businesses. They're a great place to hide.

BUSINESS STAGE: DECLINE + EMPLOYEE AGE: 50s AND 60s

Roles: Won't Be There Long Enough to Have Any

It's hard to tell who's more desperate: the declining company, or the 50- and 60-year-olds who go to work there. You may be asking yourself: *Why would anybody that age go to work for that kind of company? Why would that company hire people in that age group?* The answer is the same for both questions: They're desperate.

Let's start with the employees. They're looking for a paycheck. It's that simple. They need money and they'll work in a desperate environment if that's what it takes to get it.

The company isn't any better. It needs faces and hands. If this is the best they can do, they'll hire these people.

Unfortunately, this union will be short-lived. The company needs employees who will work night and day to save its bacon. That's generally not going to happen with this group. They want to work their forty hours or less. Preferably less. Preferably doing as little in that less as possible.

Quickly the company is going to see it isn't getting the production it needs and will say: "Don't let the door hit you on the you-know-what on your way out."

BUSINESS STAGE: DEATH + EMPLOYEE AGE: 50s AND 60s

Roles: Revisionist, Naysayer, Finger-Pointer

For the 50- and 60-year-olds still employed by the company at the time of its death, it will be all long faces and snide comments about what should have been done. After that, they'll be gone and never give the company a second thought.

+   +   +

I could have done a deeper dive into each of these categories, but I think there's enough here to give you an indication of what happens when the two life cycles collide. If you're the right person and you're in the right place, hey, it can be magical. Wrong person, wrong place, and it can be awkward, short, and ugly.

Never was any of this brought home to me more than when I visited the chairman of a start-up traditional company. He was a silver-haired smooth talker, with a firm handshake and the air of a man who had already solved most of the world's problems. His office was impressively large and impressively furnished: huge desk, high-backed leather executive chair, small conference table, and an informal seating area with two chairs and a sofa around a low coffee table.

I couldn't help but notice there wasn't one piece of paper on his desk. No sales figures. No quarterly statements. No inventory sheets. No work in progress (WIP). No memos. Nothing. In fact, the only things on his desk were a silver-framed picture of his wife, a really fancy pen set, and an executive toy (the one with the swinging balls that hit each other and go forever). That was it.

He had coffee brought in and we had a very nice talk in the informal seating area about what his company could do for ours. But, you know, it was all smooth talk and platitudes. His mind was a lot like his desk. He didn't know much about the company he was representing. He was a face. A handshake.

It took me another meeting to lose him and find someone who actually knew something. Turned out it was a 29-year-old kid.

You probably have similar stories. Now's a great time to dust them off and think about them as they apply to your business.

Exercises:

☑ As the CEO/owner of a traditional business, where are you in the combined business/personal life cycle? What could you do to make your situation/the company's situation better?

☑ Where are your key managers in the combined business/personal life cycle? Plot out each member of your executive team. It may be an eye-opener.

☑ How could changes in the business/personal life cycle positively impact your business? Make a list. Which are the most important? How hard will they be to implement?

CHAPTER 7

ZOMBIES IN THE OFFICE

Earlier, we determined that no business is completely immune from zombies. Even if you don't have any now, you might inadvertently hire one. Or an employee could become infected on the job and become one. That's why we must all be eternally vigilant.

Part of that vigilance requires knowing where zombies are likely to appear in the business/personal life cycle. They pop up in all sorts of places, but the sad truth is that **zombies congregate in the life cycles that are the most crucial to traditional businesses: growth, maturity, and decline.** See Figure 7.1.

Understanding the cycles and how zombies take advantage of them can spell the difference between a mature traditional business sliding into decline or rising into growth.

Here are examples. *(Spoiler alert: They aren't pretty. But they are thought provoking.)*

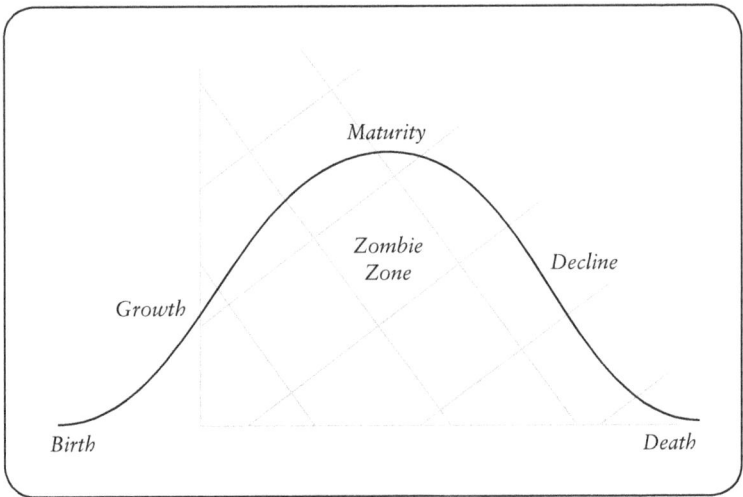

Figure 7.1 Where Zombies Congregate

GROWTH

Greta's Brownies

Greta had been a foodie since she was a small child. She really never met a food she didn't like, but if pressed to say what her favorite food might be, she'd shyly say: "chocolate."

In fact, she was known for her chocolate brownies. Every time she brought them to company functions, everyone raved about them. When Greta left the company to care for her mother, one of her workmates suggested that if she wanted to work from home, she should make brownies.

Greta didn't take the idea seriously until one of the company's VPs called her at home and asked her to make brownies for a party he was planning.

Over the next six months, driven by word of mouth, business

picked up to the point that Greta was baking and delivering brownies five or six times a week. In fact, business grew to the point where she had to hire a neighbor girl to help her.

At tax time, her CPA sat her down and tried to help her make her home business more businesslike. His timing couldn't have been better, because Greta had been approached by a ladies boutique about selling her brownies in their store.

With this additional business, the neighborhood girl was no longer enough help and Greta hired her first full-time employee, Jean.

Jean was a godsend. She had just the right touch, and in a blind taste test, you couldn't tell Jean's brownies from Greta's. With the two of them now baking, business prospered and a small grocery chain started carrying Greta's brownies.

Greta had made, in round numbers, $1,000 in her first year of business.

With the boutique selling her brownies, her annual sales jumped to $16,000.

Fast-forward five years: Greta's operation was no longer in her home but in a commercial bakery. Her brownies were being sold in regional grocery chains and scattered boutiques. Her income was $700,000 a year. Jean was no longer with her, but Greta had a staff of twelve.

Sales were steadily increasing and after a guest spot on a national morning show, where the hostess confessed Greta's brownies were one of her guilty pleasures, demand went through the roof.

Greta added two more bakers: Tiffany and Anne. Anne was in her 40s; Tiffany, a young 20.

While Tiffany had gushed at the interview about how much

she loved cooking, especially baking—she hated the kitchen. She only took the job to get away from her parents.

On the job, Tiffany was lackadaisical. Getting ingredients in the right proportions seemed like a lot of bother. So she didn't.

The first batch of brownies with a strange taste turned up in Tennessee.

After the store had several customers bring the product back, they pulled all Greta's brownies from the shelves, and told Greta they weren't going to carry her product anymore.

Concerned that her quality control had failed her, Greta mother-henned the bakers, which really ticked Tiffany off. After all, she didn't need somebody standing over her shoulder, correcting her, and telling her what to do every second. It was annoying. So annoying, she thought a little revenge might be in order. So she dropped three paperclips, one each in different batches of brownies.

The first paperclip was discovered by a woman in Pittsburg, PA, and her story ran on the local TV channel's six and eleven o'clock news. The second paperclip turned up in Columbus, OH, and it, too, made the evening news. By the time the third paperclip surfaced in Evansville, IN, Greta's business was ruined. TV media had linked the first two incidents and stories were all over the Internet.

Greta was in tears.

Being a zombie, Tiffany couldn't have cared less. It was just a job, and a stupid one at that.

Questions:

☑ Earlier, we talked about how most 20- and 30-year-olds want to make their mark in the world. Why do you think Tiffany was different? And why did she exhibit such zombie-like behavior?

☑ Tiffany's interview fooled Greta. What more could Greta have done to make sure she was hiring an honorable person?

☑ Tiffany's act of revenge was sparked by Greta's mother-henning the bakers. How much supervision is enough, and how much is too much?

MATURITY

Len's Painting and Siding Business

Len, a short, paunchy, bald man with a ready smile and quip, was the second-generation owner of a mature home-services company with several divisions—siding, painting, and gutters. Len's father and uncle started the company in 1957 to do residential and commercial painting.

At Len's uncle's urging, the company added siding in 1985. It was a natural line extension, since many of the homes the company painted were frame and in poor repair.

In 1994, Len's uncle retired, followed in 1997 by Len's dad. Len bought the company that same year.

In 2000, Len added gutters to the company's offerings. The three product lines were complementary, and sales were good but tapering slightly going into the 2008 recession. As the recession lingered, Len's growth slowed and the firm had several flat years in a row.

Len noticed one of his competitors advertising "whole house refurbishment." This company could do painting, siding, gutters, and something Len's company didn't—roofing. Len knew that each time the company had added a new product line in the past, sales had increased. He became convinced he needed to add roofing.

Len called a meeting of his three managers—Steve (who had been his dad's paint crew chief and now ran the painting operations), Frank (who ran the siding crews), and Andy (who was in charge of gutters)—and shared with them his idea about adding roofing. All agreed it was a sound addition to their current offerings.

What Len didn't share with them, at this point, was who would run the new division. Len had been courting a roofer to join the company and be in charge, but the roofer wanted more than Len was willing to pay and the deal fell through.

Frustrated by the experience and not wanting to go through finding another outsider, Len took another look at his three managers.

Steve, age 58, was a hard worker who had been a painter since high school. Everyone in the company respected him and he ran his operation with tough love. Len suspected the painting operation would fall to pieces if Steve moved over to roofing. There was also no strong number two to take Steve's place, something Len recognized was a problem he'd have to correct. Len decided to leave Steve in place.

Frank, who ran siding, was 38, recently married, with two

small stepchildren. Frank had a hard-nosed work ethic and was a stickler for detail. There were seldom any complaints about the quality of the company's siding jobs, and Frank had grown siding into the company's most profitable division. There was only one downside to Frank. As much as Len hated to admit it, Frank wasn't very smart. It took him a long time and a lot of trial and error before he was comfortable doing a task. Once he was comfortable, he was fine; but until then . . . watch out. Len didn't think he could afford—nor would customers permit—the kind of OJT Frank needed to find his groove with roofing.

That left Andy, who was in charge of gutters. Andy was 55 and had the least seniority of the three. Len had bought Andy's small roofing and gutter business, so Andy did have some roofing experience. That was the plus. The negative was that Andy's division—gutters—was the lowest performing of the three. He had the fewest projects, the lowest contribution margin (net income returned to the company), and the most customer complaints. (Andy contended that it was just the nature of the gutter business—it didn't have the customer value that painting or siding enjoyed, and thus received fewer profits and more griping from customers.) Despite the negatives, Len thought Andy was his best choice. He reasoned that Andy had roofing experience, had time to take on the roofing division (unlike Steve and Frank, Andy spent a lot of time in his office); and if Len had to, he could have someone else take over gutters, freeing up Andy to handle roofing full time.

Len sat on this decision while he closed out yet another flat year. Gross income was slightly up, but expenses were up even more. Profit after taxes would be considerably less. Len astutely knew if he didn't do something to bump sales, he was going to have to cut staff to lower expenses. He was right on the edge. He had to make roofing work.

On January 1, Len made the announcement that the company was adding roofing and that Andy would lead the roofing team. He gave Andy a nice salary increase, told him he had the authority to make the division a winner, scheduled a bimonthly meeting to monitor progress, and reiterated his goal that Andy would have roofing up and running within three months.

At the first bimonthly meeting, Len was surprised to learn Andy had done nothing. Andy explained that he'd been occupied with the gutter business and hadn't had time for roofing. Len immediately gave the responsibility for gutters to someone else.

At their next meeting, Andy shared with Len that he'd scheduled trips to visit shingle suppliers and would be traveling most of the month. Len wasn't pleased by how long this was taking, but he grudgingly approved the travel.

At their next meeting, Len learned Andy hadn't selected a shingle supplier, although he was entertaining proposals. Len asked about staffing. Andy said he'd need help with that because he was too busy to do the interviews himself. (Len hired an outside company to assist.) Andy also told Len that these update meetings were taking too much of his time and they'd have to cease. Len really wasn't happy about that but agreed on the condition that Andy keep him updated via other means.

Which, of course, Andy had no intention of doing.

Len, meanwhile, was looking at his balance sheet. Painting was flat. Siding was down. Gutters had tanked. Roofing was racking up expenses against no income. The company overall was significantly down. To trim expenses, Len decided to bite the bullet and let go four employees in siding, four in painting, and one in gutters.

He explained the economic necessity of the cuts in a company-wide meeting, but employees heard a different message. Their takeaway: the company was in trouble and Len was counting on roofing to save it.

As the three-month goal approached, Andy had the staffing company select a supervisor and five workers. They made their recommendations and Andy hired them without meeting a single one.

On their first day of work, Len met the new employees and welcomed them to the company. They looked a little "rough," but roofing isn't pretty work and Len didn't voice his concerns.

Earlier, Len had done a cross-marketing promotion for roofing to the company's existing customers and had three jobs lined up.

The new crew, in a new truck purchased just for roofing, arrived at the first job. Tear-off went well. Roof went on. Job was finished on time. The crew moved on to job two.

Len got the angry call from customer one the following day. The rows of shingles were on a slant—the whole roof looked askew. The customer said he wasn't paying and expected them to fix their mistake. Len went to Andy, but Andy couldn't meet with him because he was dealing with an emergency—one of the crew had fallen off the roof at job two.

Len was beside himself.

Andy was nonchalant. "Hey, it's going to be okay," he assured Len.

Job two finished on time, even with one crew member in the hospital, and the crew moved on to job three.

Len held his breath waiting for a phone call from Andy about the injured worker. But none came.

The call came from job three instead. The customer was irate that they were installing a shingle other than the one he had chosen. "The two aren't even close," the wife complained.

Len went to Andy to halt the job, but Mother Nature beat him to it. Thunderstorms had rolled into the area.

Len's phone went crazy. Customer two was calling to say her roof was leaking in multiple places. Customer three was calling to say his roof hadn't been tarped to protect the areas already torn off and that water was streaming in. He finished with an emphatic, "You'll hear from my lawyer!"

The carnage was pretty horrific. Len figured he had no choice. He fired Andy and the entire roofing crew.

He had to hire an outside roofing company to redo house one and house two.

Customer three took him to court and won a judgment against him.

Len learned that Andy had done little—other than making his trips to the shingle manufacturers—but stay in his office and play online poker. It turned out he'd gotten addicted to it while running the gutter division.

In court, the attorney for the homeowner revealed that Andy's crew had two members with prison records and one who had failed three straight drug tests. Again, Andy hadn't bothered to check.

His company's reputation in tatters, Len was devastated, both personally and financially. He'd expected roofing to lift the company's fortunes; instead he had to drain his 401(k) to stave off bankruptcy.

If you ask him, Len humbly takes the blame for everything that happened. Many in the company think Len did everything right, that his only mistake was Andy. When Len looks back, though, he remembers that his focus on growth and his simplistic approach to the risk were the errors. And, of course, his neglecting to keep better watch on the performance of his employees—perhaps conducting annual reviews or, at the very least, forcing himself to take a long, hard look at every employee in his company. Instead he assumed if he'd hired the person, that person must be great. Len now realizes that if you combine hubris (assuming you've done everything right, and don't need to rethink, say, hiring decisions) with zombie-like behavior, you get turbo zombie.

And if you put that turbo zombie in charge of something important, it will be enough to do you in, big time.

Questions:

☑ Of Steve, Frank, and Andy, who would you have tapped to run roofing? Or would you have continued the outside search?

☑ Andy was 55. Do you think that played into Andy's poor performance? Should Len have had a series of talks with Andy about whether he had the drive to take on a major responsibility?

☑ Andy was pretty much "retired on the job." How might Len have realized this sooner, and what might he have done to correct it?

DECLINE

Tom's Plumbing Business

A large plumbing company that worked mostly for homebuilders needed to fill three vacancies on its plumbing staff. The company had bled red ink all through the housing downturn, but with home start-ups, management was hoping for a reversal of fortunes. The company interviewed a number of plumbers and, based on experience and face-to-face interviews, selected three men: Jacob (29 years old), Ernie (55 years old), and Charles (oldest at 61).

The company had two clients putting up subdivisions of market homes. The influx of new blood and seasoned experience was supposed to get the plumbing work back on schedule. Rough-ins were behind, and the other subs were complaining that they were being delayed. Tom, the owner of the plumbing company, personally assured both builders they'd see the situation improve quickly.

What Tom didn't realize—what a lot of employers don't realize, because it can be impossible to spot until the damage has begun—was that he'd hired three zombies. Here's how it played out.

Jacob and his wife, a dental hygienist, had three boys, ages 9, 7, and 2-and-a-half. Because his wife couldn't leave work, Jacob picked the boys up from school, took them to after-school care, and, as if that weren't enough, coached the two older boys' soccer teams. His life revolved around taking care of the boys. He often arrived to work late (due to a slowdown in the school drop-off line), frequently talked on his cell about child-related issues, and left early to get to games.

Jacob's work, when he was there, was good. But he wasn't there enough. Tom was hoping he'd work fifty hours a week to help get them over the hump. Jacob, however, was working far less—maybe thirty-five or thirty-six—and approaching his tasks like it was a second, less important job.

When other workers called out Jacob on not doing his share, he blew them off, saying they didn't know what their real priorities were. A couple of the other plumbers agreed with him and slowed down, too.

Jacob's work fell further and further behind. Tom finally called him into the office to find out why. Jacob gave him a lot of not-my-fault excuses, and Tom gave him the benefit of the doubt. Mistake. A week later, the client was furious at the slow progress and told Tom if three houses weren't finished in the next five days, Tom would be fired. At that moment Tom wished he'd fired Jacob and replaced him, but now with this deadline, he thought he had to keep him on.

Tom pulled plumbers off other jobs and had them concentrate on these houses.

Unfortunately, two of those plumbers were Ernie and Charlie.

For Ernie, who was working at a different builder's subdivision, the commute would be a half-hour longer. He didn't want to make the drive, so he told his current builder that Tom was pulling him off his project. That caused Ernie's builder to call Tom and yell, "Absolutely unacceptable!" As a result of the call, Tom had no choice but to let Ernie and two other plumbers continue back at their original site.

Charlie was worse. When Tom reassigned him, he saw some intense work coming, wanted no part of it, and filed a worker's comp claim, saying he'd hurt his back.

Jacob, meanwhile, decided he wasn't going to put in the hours, left a voicemail for Tom saying he quit, and as a going-away present, dumped a liter of Mountain Dew in the gas tank of the company truck.

So, let's take stock here. Three hires. Three self-centered individuals who were totally out for themselves. That certainly qualifies as zombie behavior.

The result: Tom's company didn't finish the five houses in time, and he was fired from the project. The other builder, unhappy with Ernie's work, fired Tom three weeks later.

Tom immediately tried to rightsize the company, but he was taking on too much water. His was no longer a declining company; it was a plummeting company. In three months, it flatlined. Tom was in chapter 7 and out of business.

There's no definitive way to say, but Tom believes those three zombie hires were the difference between getting back in the black and being out of business.

I have to agree with him. While you can't walk a company's death back to one person or one event, you can with some certainty see where things started to go south. Or in Tom's case, to go south even faster.

Questions:

☑ Obviously, Tom's company was desperate to get client work finished. What should Tom have done with his new hires to protect himself in this situation?

☑ Jacob was 29. Ernie was 55. Charles was 61. What should Tom have expected from workers at that age? What did he get? How could he have gotten more from each of these men?

☑ Was there any investment by Jacob, Ernie, or Charles in Tom's business? How could there have been?

+   +   +

My point with all three of these stories is that keeping a traditional business growing or shifting it back into growth mode is difficult enough without zombies sabotaging your hard work. As we've seen, one zombie—*one*—can undo everything.

As we talk about how to promote growth, we're also going to talk about zombie-proofing your business.

Exercises:

☑ Everyone has experienced situations like these. Thinking back, what were yours? Were you the victim of zombie behavior?

☑ What could you have done to deal with the problem employee(s)? How would that have changed the outcome?

CHAPTER 8

LET'S TALK ABOUT GROWTH

By now you are probably saying: *Okay, Jamie, this life cycle/ zombie stuff is interesting and all, but how in blue blazes is it going to help me grow my traditional business?*

The answer is pretty simple. This is information you need to succeed if you want to do any of these things:

- Keep a growing traditional business growing.

- Help a mature traditional business grow instead of sliding into decline.

- Reverse the fortunes of a declining traditional business and start it growing again.

Being able to identify your current situation and instituting a common language to talk about it is a first step in crafting a solution. Once you have that, the following steps become easier. That's important, because I want this to be understandable and encouraging. I don't want to make it as complicated as directions for assembling a bicycle.

Let's take these steps one at a time.

KEEPING A GROWING BUSINESS GROWING

When your traditional business is in growth mode and things are going great, you feel invincible. You've figured out the winning formula and you're confident that if you continue doing what you're doing, you'll continue to enjoy growth.

You couldn't be more wrong.

Here's why: **What made you a success isn't necessarily what will make you a success moving forward.**

I see you shaking your head and saying, *No, no! Say it's not so!*

I feel your pain. It's a lot easier to keep doing what you've been doing than to embrace constant change, but here's the thing: by embracing change, you'll be looking forward rather than rubberstamping the past.

Remember earlier when we talked about how traditional companies—because they're repetitive businesses—get into a rhythm, that rhythm becomes a routine, and that routine becomes a religion? That religion actually reinforces the notion that if you keep doing what you're doing, you'll continue to be successful.

Because traditional businesses are so repetitive—with each year a virtual carbon copy of the last—I believe we're more susceptible to people and events that can quickly truncate the growth curve.

Let's look at an example.

Mr. Personalization

Larry, age 59, was the owner of a direct mail house he'd started thirty years earlier. His claim to fame was personalization. You've seen those mailers. It's the advertisement that arrives in your mailbox announcing, *James Gerdsen, look inside. You could win a NEW car!* Except it would be your name, not mine.

Personalization was all the rage for a while because direct mail results were better with it. Significantly better. People liked seeing their name on things. And Larry had all the printing equipment, technology, and staff to do personalization right. Each year, he would attend trade shows to find out what the latest advance in personalization might be. He never skimped. Whatever was bright and shiny, he bought.

And it worked for him. He had a run of eleven years where his business—built on personalization—grew every year. Clients complimented him on his work. Even other direct mail houses allowed: If you want personalization, Larry's your guy.

But Larry let personalization give him tunnel vision. He wasn't watching what else was happening that might impact his business. When social media came along, Larry summarily dismissed it as *that fad my grandkids like.* He even badmouthed it to clients. So when social media really took off, business went everywhere but to Larry.

Social media was the outside force that flattened Larry's

growth curve. If he had been thinking of what would make him successful in the future versus what had worked for him in the past, he might not have missed the wave.

But Larry had one other thing working against him. At age 59, he was in semi-retirement mode. He didn't want to exert the energy to learn about something new. He was his own worst zombie.

Ms. Third-Generation Sports Store Owner

Jessica was the third-generation owner of a sporting goods store. Her grandfather founded the store when his career playing minor league baseball ended. Jessica and her father before her were both big supporters of local youth teams. They sponsored them, took ads in programs, and helped refurbish fields. They were good people who were genuinely beloved by the community.

Their store was in an older three-story building in the local business district that hadn't changed much since Jessica's grandfather's day.

Jessica had six employees, no debt, and had grown the business nicely. She'd added running shoes, gotten into exercise equipment, and most recently had expanded the ladies' exercise apparel section. She was talking about adding personal training and offering classes in yoga, Pilates, and spinning.

But that never happened.

Jessica remembers she was watching a Little League game (one of the youth teams the store sponsored) when she first heard the news that a big-box sporting goods store was going to open outside of town. That worried her. Worried her a lot. But she assumed her customers would stay loyal—after all, hadn't the store loyally supported the community for three generations?

When the big-box store opened, though, more than half of Jessica's business disappeared overnight. Loyalty? *Ha.* The big-box store had lower prices and a bigger selection. Jessica hung on for as long as she could—almost a year—before she had to close the store.

Jessica's is the classic story of the mom-and-pop business doing wonderfully until a big outside player enters the market. Although she'd kept the business growing, that big-box did a big number on it. She was totally blindsided. She'd never thought anyone would enter her market, much less take away so much of her business.

+   +   +

Both of these traditional businesses were victims of change. Larry probably could have saved his business if he hadn't been so myopic, but poor Jessica had no chance. The big-box store had resources she simply couldn't match.

Ms. Sandwich Shop and Her Staff

Nancy opened a downtown sandwich shop that catered to the noontime business crowd. The menu was double-decker sandwiches and soups. Both pretty darn tasty and value priced. For five years, the shop grew each year to the point where during every lunchtime, lines of people would be waiting for a seat.

Nancy worked in the back watching over the kitchen. Out

front, she had a young hostess, Melody, who managed the queue and showed patrons to their tables. Melody was one of those people who could light up a room. She knew all the regulars by name, asked about their spouses or children, and made the sometimes-lengthy wait for a table not so bad.

Melody went to Nancy and asked for a raise. Nancy bristled at that. Money was tight, and because Nancy hadn't given herself a raise in a long time, she didn't think it would be fair to give one to Melody. Nancy thought about all the hours she put into the restaurant business. She had to get up early to go to the market and buy items for the day's luncheon; she had to arrive early and open the store. She was the one who had to deal with health inspectors, building management, and all the rest.

What did Melody do? Smile, and hand out menus. How hard was that?

In the end, Nancy gave her hostess the teeny, tiniest of raises, which hurt Melody's feelings by making her feel like she wasn't a valued asset.

Melody quickly found another job that paid more. Nancy hired a replacement, but she wasn't as personable as Melody and she didn't have the same history with the regulars.

Business dropped way off. It took Nancy two more hires for that position before she found another Melody.

This, I believe, is the shoot-yourself-in-the-foot way to flatten your growth curve. Always remember, it's not just you—the CEO/owner—who makes a business grow. Your key staffers—who interact with your customers—play a huge part in that. Losing one may be a change that hurts.

+   +   +

So far, we've talked about three factors—changes in technology, outside competition, loss of key staff—that can derail growth. There are many more. Here are a few of the most common factors:

- **Changes by the manufacturer:** If you are a value-added reseller and the manufacturer changes the line you carry or eliminates line items, it may weaken the relationship you have with your customers.

- **Product recalls:** If stock you carry is subject to a recall, by either the manufacturer or a regulatory body, customers may shift to competitive products. Once they shift, they might not come back.

- **Population shift:** Your store or service may be located in a high-demand area, but if the population shifts, the demand may move with it.

- **Acts of God:** No company is ever prepared for the devastation caused by a fire, flood, or other natural disaster. You can lose your inventory, your accounts receivable, even the names of your customers. Insurance will help, but frankly, it's a financial Band-Aid. The real damage is that your energy is focused on rebuilding rather than on your customers.

- **Health issues:** Often overlooked, health issues have a way of doing insidious damage. While the owner is recuperating from triple bypass surgery, who's left running the business, making timely decisions? What's that owner going to be like when he returns? His old self? Or a timid shadow of his former self?

• **Bad word of mouth:** Just as good buzz can help a business, bad buzz can be a killer. Competitors or customers with an ax to grind can use social media like a billy club. All it takes is one bad rumor that goes viral and—even if it isn't true—your reputation can be ruined.

So what can you do to help your growing business keep growing? Plan. Plan. And plan some more.

Here's how I recommend you approach this.

It helps if you have a large whiteboard or, better yet, a whole room that you can dedicate as a war room. Because that's what we're going to be doing here—waging a war that preempts the negative effects of change.

In essence, we're going to be doing an exercise like a SWAT analysis—strengths, weaknesses, advantages, and threats. But with a traditional business, we need to change the analysis somewhat, because many of the strengths you'd probably list are also threats.

How can something be both?

Easier than you think. Let's take the concept of each year being very much like the last. Many businesses would consider that a strength, but for traditional business it is also a threat because it can lull you into missing what's going on around you.

Because strengths and threats are two sides of the same coin, we're going to deep-six SWAT and work with a more usable analysis model—PEP. PEP is as good an acronym as SWAT, maybe even better. PEP stands for people, experience, and products.

Why are these three things more important than SWAT? Easy, they're not about you; they're more about your customers—which is where the emphasis needs to be. Remember, you may have or at least think you have the best product or service in the world, but if your customers don't believe it, well, what do you really have?

The customer experience is a game changer and we need to recognize that, quit spending so much time talking about ourselves, and spend more time thinking about our customers.

THE POWER OF PEP: PEOPLE, EXPERIENCE, AND PRODUCTS

Every traditional business can benefit from learning how to fulfill the needs of the customer. Get ready to create some more charts.

People

We're going to start with the first P—people. For this P, I want you to create a depth chart for your company. You've seen these charts before. You, as CEO/owner, are at the top. Your direct reports are under you. Their direct reports under them. My recommendation is to use a 3-by-5-inch index card for each person in your organization, which you can then arrange in org chart form.

On each of these cards, list the person's name, age, title, responsibility, and strengths and weaknesses. (Strengths and weaknesses will be things like: Idea generator. Handles large amounts of detail well. Poor social skills. Always late.)

Put the cards in place on your whiteboard or wall. Once they're in place, I want you to look at your organization from the following perspectives.

The Company Perspective:

- How do you feel about your organization overall? Do you have the right people in the right places? If so, congratulations. If not, is there training that will make this person or persons more effective? Are there people who need to be replaced? Are there people who are "aging out"?

- Who in the organization is driving growth? Next to the name of any individual you believe is crucial to continued growth, pencil in a "G." How can you leverage this person to create even more growth?

- Do you see holes in the organization that require adding a position or positions? If so, what kind of person would be most effective in this slot?

Now that you've looked at your organization from the company's viewpoint, pretend you are a customer and look at the organization from the customer's perspective.

The Customer Perspective:

- Are the people who interface with the customer the right people for those roles? Do they have the right kind of support to deliver genuinely awesome customer service? If so, put a plan in place to reward those people. If not, what can you do to improve your level of customer service?

- Thinking from the customer's perspective, would adding a position or positions improve the customer experience? If so, what kind of person would be most effective in this slot?

Earlier, you looked at the organization overall. Now I want you to look at each individual within the organization.

The Individual Perspective:

- By each person's name, pencil in an "I" if the person is invested in the organization or an "N" if not invested. If there are some individuals who are questionable, mark them as "N." If you're not certain whether a particular individual is invested, chances are that person is not. Now I want you to circle—again in pencil—each person's age.

In effect, what we're doing is a zombie scan. This is a quick test to see if zombies are in your organization or you're about to become a zombie breeding ground. Individuals who aren't invested in your company have a high likelihood of being or becoming zombies. Individuals in the older age brackets may retire on the job, becoming zombies and infecting others. Combine the two—not invested and older age—and your zombie chances skyrocket.

+   +   +

So, you just took three looks at the organization: How you feel about your people. How your customers see your organization. And where trouble spots may be or may develop. With these in hand, we're ready to move on to E—experience.

Experience

Earlier I talked about the customer experience being a game changer. I wasn't exaggerating a bit. You can have the best product and the best people, but if the customer experience is lousy, people will take their business elsewhere.

Think about Internet sites. The ones that have a good customer experience—load quickly, have intuitive architecture, are easy to navigate, have secure shopping, and confirm your transaction quickly—are the ones you return to. Why? Simple. They've made it easy for you to like them.

Bricks-and-mortar businesses are the same way. Some make it easy for you to do business with them. Some seem to do everything possible to drive you away.

Quick story.

Last fall, I had a raccoon in my attic. I could hear him roaming around at night. Now, I'm not afraid of much, but I had no desire to tangle with this raccoon. So the next morning, I googled "Pest Removal." Since I didn't know any of these companies, I called the first one on the list.

I got voicemail. "Leave a message; we'll get back to you." Great. When? I'm in kind of a hurry here.

Second name on the list, second call. Voicemail again: "Sorry we're not in right now, but if this is an emergency call this number." I immediately called that number and it rang and rang. Fifty rings. No one picked up. So much for emergency service.

Third name, third call. Got a live person. I was thrilled. She listened to my problem, commiserated with me, but had no idea when one of their crews might be able to trap my raccoon.

Fourth name, fourth call. A man—sounded like he was on his cell—answered. Sure enough, he'd taken the call in his truck. I explained my problem. He summarized what he'd do to deal with my raccoon, let me know his fee was $150, and said he could be at my house in forty minutes.

Of course, I hired him. He'd made it easy for me to buy.

+   +   +

Let's see how easy *you* make it for your customers.

To do this experience analysis, I want you to create a schematic of a typical customer interaction. Never built a schematic before? Piece of cake. It's going to be a lot of squares connected by lines. Here's an example of how you do it.

Let's say customer requests come to your business either over the phone or via the web to a central customer response center. Create a square for each of these places marked "Phone First Contact" or "Web First Contact" and connect them to a square marked "Customer Response Center/Headquarters."

The Customer Response Center/Headquarters takes the customer information, schedules an appointment (let's say in this case it's an emergency), and informs the first available "Service

Professional." For this step, draw a line from Customer Response Center/Headquarters to a new square marked Service Professional.

Now it gets interesting. When the Service Professional goes to the customer's location, will he have the parts and equipment on board his truck to perform the service? Or will he have to come back to the shop for needed parts? For the sake of the example, let's say he doesn't have all the parts on his truck, so he's going to have to leave the customer's location, return to the shop, get what he needs, and return to the customer's location. That means we've got a bunch of squares and lines to draw. One line from the Service Professional to "Customer Location," one line from Customer Location to Customer Response Center/Headquarters, and another one back to Customer Location.

The two schematics would look something like Figures 8.1 and 8.2.

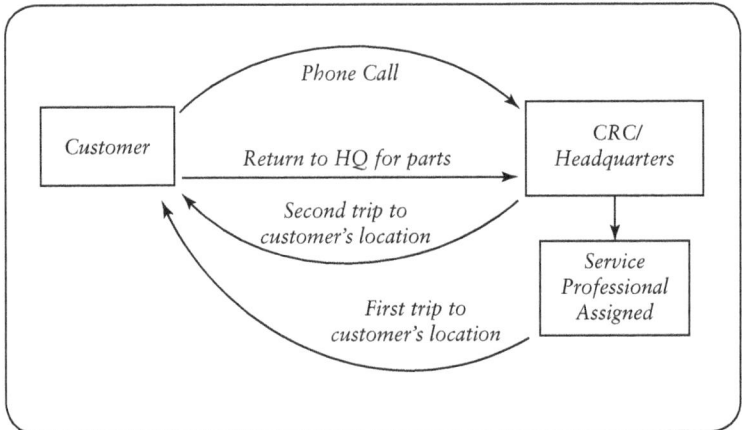

Figure 8.1 Customer Interaction Schematic NOT ALL Parts on Truck

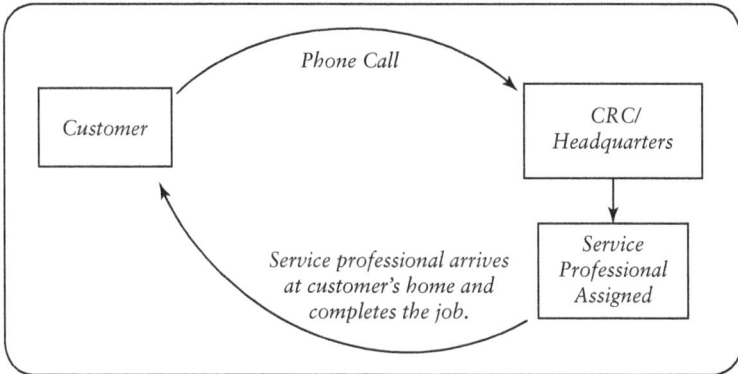

Figure 8.2 *Customer Interaction Schematic ALL Parts on Truck*

Now I'd like you to put estimated times next to the lines for each step. For example, Phone First Contact to Customer Response Center/Headquarters is five minutes. Customer Response Center/Headquarters to Service Professional is twelve minutes. And so on.

And one final thing, put a star on each step in which there is customer contact. Your schematic would look something like Figure 8.3.

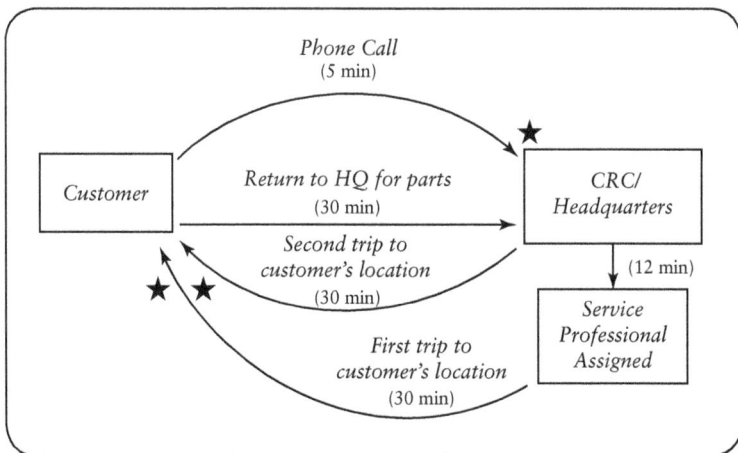

Figure 8.3 *Customer Interaction Schematic NOT ALL Parts on Truck.*
Total time: 1 hr. 47 min.

Good. You've done it. You've created a schematic of a typical service call, identified the points of customer contact, and determined a time frame. With this key information to use as a baseline, we can see if—and how—the customer experience can be improved. See Figure 8.4 for the better version of this particular customer interaction.

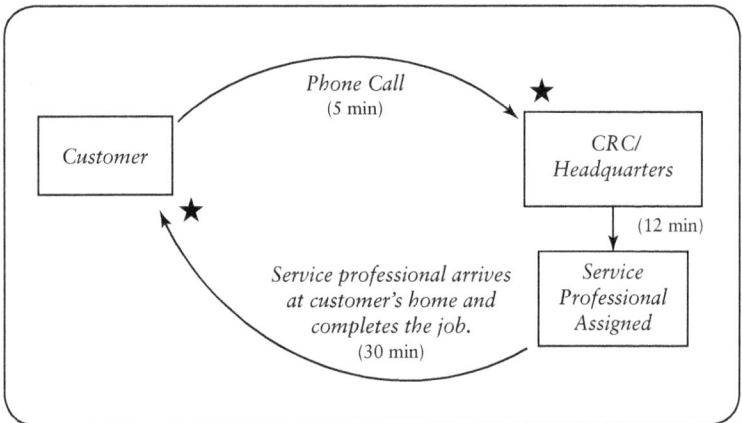

Figure 8.4 *Customer Interaction Schematic ALL Parts on Truck.*
Total time: 47 min.

Why is this so important? Because anything that makes the customer experience better makes you more valuable to the customer. That's just common sense.

Evaluating the customer experience to see how it can be made better is called continuous improvement. There's a whole body of literature about how to use continuous improvement to make operations more efficient and customer focused. (The Japanese have a word for this ongoing fine-tuning to improve, streamline, and standardize every function within a business: "*kaizen.*"

Search the Internet for fascinating examples of how companies around the world have put the principles of *kaizen* to use.)

We're going to look at the schematic we've created through the lens of continuous improvement and apply *kaizen* to see where we can extract inefficiencies.

The early part of our schematic, from Phone First Contact to Customer Location, looks good—there's no inefficiency in how these steps are handled. However, the part where the tech has to return to the Customer Response Center/Headquarters and then back to the Customer Location is a problem. It inconveniences the customer and requires more of the professional's time. This could have been avoided if the professional's truck had been stocked with the most commonly needed parts.

So let's say we make this change and stock more on the trucks. On our schematic, eliminate that inefficient step of returning from the Customer Location to Customer Response Center/Headquarters for parts and going back to the Customer Location. Isn't this now a simpler process? We've eliminated nonproductive time, allowing our professionals to spend more of their time working with customers. But more importantly, by eliminating the need to go back to the shop for parts—which is potentially irritating to the customer—we've created a better customer experience.

This is just a simple example. But look at your entire organization with a continuous improvement mindset. You might be surprised at how many improvements you see. And don't think this is some crackpot exercise, either. Many organizations, including Toyota, have embraced *kaizen*, and I have to say, once you see how much better these continuous improvements make your company, you'll be a *kaizen* advocate.

Products

Our last P is for products. Many traditional businesses are value-added resellers, so products are vitally important. At my HVAC business, Apollo, we sell different brands of furnaces and air conditioners. We offer the lines we do because we've researched the manufacturers and believe they offer the best value to our customers. Now, HVAC systems are not fancy-schmancy branded products. Most customers couldn't tell you the brand of furnace or air conditioner in their home. For hot water heaters it's even worse.

Consumers trust their service provider to supply them with long-lasting, quality products. It's a responsibility we take very seriously at Apollo. We're constantly looking for products that offer added energy efficiency or have a simpler design so there's less wear on the unit.

We also take the time to try and share this knowledge with our customers. A new furnace shouldn't be a mystery box. You should know the improvements that have been added since your last furnace and know the efficiency you're gaining.

As a growth business, you should be actively reviewing your core product offering and you should be looking for line extension products. My favorite example of line extension is Mr. Clean from P&G. It started out as a liquid cleaner. Now there are more products under the Mr. Clean name, including Mr. Clean Magic Erasers and even Mr. Clean Car Washes. Line extenders are like growth extenders. Watch for them.

Products often get blamed for a traditional business's shortcomings in either people or experience. When people talk about why a business failed, the answer is inevitably product.

I couldn't disagree more.

Usually, it's the people who failed the product. And because the people failed, the experience tanked. But all that's complicated. Blaming product is way easier. That's why it happens way more.

+   +   +

I encourage you to spend time with PEP. When you put the three parts together, you have a diagnostic for growth health.

If you have the right **people** in place, you should deliver a good customer experience and should have sought out the right products and services.

If you have a good customer **experience**, you'll retain customers and have the opportunity to do additional work.

If the **products** support the customer experience, it deepens and reinforces that experience.

Additionally, using PEP as a diagnostic will keep you from relying too heavily on the rearview mirror. Remember what we said earlier: **What made your business a success in the past isn't necessarily what will make it a success moving forward.** PEP can make sure you're addressing the factors that are important to continued success.

Exercises:

☑ Find a space inside your organization to use as a war room. This can be a whiteboard or an entire room where you put things on the walls. It's important that you have all the necessary tools available—paper, markers, reports, whatever you need—so that you're able to write what's needed without any delays or distractions.

☑ Create employee profile cards and begin to build a process/organizational chart. Be meticulous with your annotations. Do you have the right people in the right places? Are there people you need to move to make the organization more efficient? Are there additional positions that need to be added to improve your customer experience?

☑ Create a schematic of how your company handles a typical customer call. Once you have the schematic, apply the continual-improvement principles of *kaizen* to see where you can eliminate inefficiencies. How will the changes you make improve your customer experience?

☑ If you have a management team you trust, consider involving them in discussions about using the principles of *kaizen*. This often functions well as a group exercise, and it gives them "buy in" to the process changes.

☑ Review your product line to see if you're up to date with the latest in your field. Are there line extensions you should be considering? Are there related products that would create ancillary sales?

CHAPTER 9

HELPING A MATURE BUSINESS GROW INSTEAD OF DECLINE

If you think it's hard to keep a growing business growing, prepare yourself. All the things that bedevil the growing business—outside competition, management issues, population shift, to name just a few—are worse for a mature business. Think of it like the flu. A younger adult (growing business) usually bounces back quickly from a case of the flu. For an older adult (mature business), the flu may last longer and may even prove fatal.

So, a mature traditional business must:

- Deal with problems that might send it into decline, and

- Dial up the factors that propel growth.

It would be nice if we could just jump to the factors that propel growth and not worry about decline problems, but in my experience, that's wishful thinking. In fact, I'd liken it to building a house on a cracked foundation. You can do it, but it's going to be harder, and those cracks will eventually cause structural problems that are difficult and expensive to repair. The PEP analysis that we talked about in the previous chapter can give you a sense of the number and depth of cracks in your organizational foundation. I'd start with the first P—people. Take a hard look at all the people in your organization. And that includes you, the CEO/owner.

Granted, you built the business. You've missed family dinners, your kid's birthdays. You've worked through Christmas, haven't taken a vacation in years. Nobody questions how much you've given. In fact, your whole identity is wrapped up in that business. But has something happened so that you're no longer emotionally invested?

I can speak from experience. I had a personal issue that kept me away from the office for the better part of a year. At the time, I'd have told you I had everything under control. But I didn't. I wasn't emotionally invested. My mind was elsewhere.

A year later, I'm seeing the damage that emotional detachment caused.

So, if that's you, this is the first problem we need to address, because as the CEO/owner, you're the linchpin of success or failure.

REJUVENATING THE CEO/OWNER

Think of this as a blessing. Don't look at it as a repudiation of what you've accomplished. It's not. It's a way to jump-start the next phase of an already stellar career.

Remember, it's the repetitiveness of the traditional business that causes burnout. You've done the same things, dealt with the same problems, smoothed over the same divisive issues, year after year. It would be amazing if you didn't tire of all that.

So the question is—how do we get some of that off your plate?

There are a number of ways. Use the one that seems most appropriate for your situation.

THE HAND-OFF TO THE NEXT GENERATION

This is what worked for us at Apollo. Even before we talked about my buying the company, my dad was giving me responsibility and authority for selected functions. It freed him of tasks he was tired of and helped me get a deeper understanding of the nuances of running the company.

If the next generation is working in your business—can you hand off more to them?

I knew a family business where the owner had three sons. In preparation for retirement, he conducted a test. He gave one son responsibility for operations, another son responsibility for sales, and the third son responsibility for marketing. He wanted to see how each performed and how well they worked together. He envisioned the oldest son, the one he'd tasked with sales, to be his potential heir as CEO. But he was surprised when the middle son—the one with responsibility for operations—turned out to be the clear leader. In fact, the middle son worked with his brothers and put a more effective management organization in place—with the older brother handling R&D and new ventures and the younger brother responsible for sales and marketing. Dad saw the company humming along, stepped up to chairman, and was able to spend more time doing what he loved—restoring historic homes.

Don't have the second generation involved? Do it. I heard about a CEO who was tired of working seventy-hour weeks, so he hired three whiz kids (his name for them) and gave one of them new accounts, one current accounts, and one service. Each was given a 5 percent stake in the business with the understanding that they could buy the remaining 85 percent from him over the next ten years.

As it turned out, one left after a year. (A traditional business was just too boring for her.) One married, and his interest in the business plummeted. But the last one turned out to be a winner. He doubled current accounts, revamped service, and put an effective new accounts program in place. The CEO sold the business to him in year seven for a better figure than he'd expected.

I also know a CEO in his 60s who loved creating improvements to the tools his business used. He held three patents and wanted to spend time developing more. So he brought in a young woman as EVP, had her shadow him for a year, and then stepped back and let her run the company with minimal oversight. He was newly energized by not having to deal with day-to-day operations and by being able to work on his inventions.

As the CEO/owner, you are the controlling intelligence of the company. You set the work ethic, the pace, and the mood of your business. If you—because of age, weariness, health, or any other reason—have become un-invested in the business, this is the problem that must be fixed *first*.

The good news is: although you may be the problem, you are also the solution. As these three stories show, there are ways for you to hand off the tedious day-to-day responsibility and create a setting that will allow you to do more of what you want to do.

DEALING WITH OTHER PERSONNEL ISSUES

Earlier, in our discussion about PEP, we created a depth chart of your staff. You'll remember that, in this chart, each person had a 3-by-5-inch index card listing name, age, title, responsibility, and strengths and weaknesses.

In moving your mature company back to growth, I want you to view the chart again from three perspectives.

The Company Perspective:

- How do you feel about your organization overall? Do you have the right people in the right places? If so, congratulations. If not, is there training that will make this person or persons more effective? Are there people who need to be replaced? Are there people who are "aging out"?

- Who in the organization is driving growth? In pencil, mark a "G" next to the name of any individual you believe is crucial to continued growth. How can you leverage this person to create even more growth?

- Do you see holes in the organization that require adding a position or position? If so, what kind of person would be most effective in this slot?

The Customer Perspective:

- Next, pretend you're a customer and look at the organization from the customer's perspective: Are the people who interface with you, as customer, the right people for those roles? Do they have the right kind of support to deliver genuinely awesome customer service? If so, put a plan in place to reward those people. If not, what can you do to improve your level of customer service?

- Again, considering the customer's perspective: Would adding one or more positions improve the customer experience? If so, what kind of person would be most effective in this slot?

The Individual Perspective:

- Look closely at each individual in the organization. By each person's name I want you to pencil in an "I" if the person is invested in the organization, or "N" if *not* invested. If there are some individuals who are questionable, mark them as "N." If you're not certain if a particular individual is invested, chances are that person isn't. Now I want you to circle—again in pencil—each person's age.

In effect, what we're doing is a zombie scan. This is a quick test to see if zombies are in your organization or if you've become a zombie breeding ground. Individuals who aren't invested in your company have a high likelihood of being or becoming zombies. Individuals in the older age brackets may retire on the job, but only after becoming zombies and infecting others.

+   +   +

I'm repeating these three perspectives because they, too, are more important to a mature company than to a growing company. Having the wrong person in a key spot may slow a growing company. But in a mature company, that dicey staffing situation may throw the company into decline.

The old adage that one rotten apple can ruin the whole barrel is so true. For a traditional company that has plateaued to stay on a level path or return to growth, these personnel issues must be dealt with. I am especially concerned about any zombies that might be lurking in your company. Zombies sap the strength of a company, so we'll need to be especially vigilant in weeding them out.

Look at your depth chart. It's easy to see zombies when you know what you're looking for. These are the individuals who aren't invested in the company, exhibit poor performance, and produce few positive results. You'll want to deal with them right away.

****CAUTION****

When I say you'll want to deal with them immediately, I don't mean you should call John Doe into your office and tell him he's fired because he's a zombie. All that will do is get you sued. And by the time his lawyers are finished with you, John will own the company, which—because he's a zombie—he'll immediately run into the ground.

No, better to call John in, detail your concerns about his lack of productivity, and put him on a work evaluation plan. That way, John will have an opportunity to reinvest in the company. The prospect of being let go may be enough to bring him back from the undead. Or, if he continues to be unproductive, you've built and documented the case for dismissal.

Always try to salvage first. If that doesn't work, don't hesitate. All that will do is make the situation worse. Immediately let the individual go.

+   +   +

DEAL WITH THOSE P ISSUES NOW

I've got another anecdote about the importance of keeping the right people in the right places.

A friend of my dad's had a service manager, Stan, who was in his 60s and had been with the company for twenty-five years. Stan was definitely old-school and insisted the service techs do things his way. In his defense, Stan's way worked. There were just newer ways of doing things that were cheaper and easier.

The company had a high turnover in the tech ranks. The employees thought they weren't being allowed to do their jobs properly. The CEO knew Stan was the cause of the high turnover, but because of his friendship with Stan and Stan's long years with the organization, he did nothing about it.

The company hit a dry period. Four techs turned in their notice. Dad's friend felt the company slipping away. There's an old saying: *For things to get better, they must first get far worse.* That was the case here. Panic set in. Dad's friend finally had to deal with the Stan problem. Knowing Stan only had two years until retirement, he moved him into an operations role and promoted one of the senior techs to head service. The new guy immediately updated their service practices and morale in the organization soared. Stan? Dad's friend thought he'd be upset.

Maybe even quit. He wasn't. He didn't. At that point in his life, he just wanted a spot to carry him to retirement.

You don't have to wait for things to get worse to make them better. Begin dealing with any P (people) issues you have. It's amazing what new blood does for an organization. New ideas. New enthusiasm. New solutions. Even one quality hire can be felt throughout the entire organization.

EXPERIENCE THAT DEFINES SUCCESS

Once you have P under control, move on to E—your customer experience. Not to keep repeating myself, but this is vitally important to the mature traditional business, more important even than to the growing business. That's because the mature business is vulnerable to newcomers. If a newcomer has a better customer experience, it will begin draining customers away from your business.

Again, I would definitely recommend doing a schematic and seeing where you can introduce *kaizen* improvement in the customer experience.

The other thing I would definitely recommend is letting customers tell you what they like and don't like about your business. Get it straight from the horse's mouth. Customers love giving input to service companies, and getting that input is easier to do than you might think.

Use your customer database and send your customers, either via snail mail or email, a short questionnaire. Don't make it complicated. Don't make them write a bunch of stuff. 'Cause if you do, nobody will respond. Just ask a couple of simple questions about areas you believe are important.

For example, Apollo did a quick e-survey asking:

1. Did our techs explain the service process to the customer's satisfaction?

2. Did the customer think the tech had preformed the service quickly and efficiently?

3. Were the techs tidy and did they treat the customer's home as if it had been their own?

Hey, three simple questions. Anybody's willing to answer three questions. Ask three each quarter and suddenly you're getting some significant feedback.

If we'd gotten customers who said: "Your guys are messy. You left our basement a wreck." Well, then we know we have a customer experience problem to fix.

I mentioned snail mail and email questionnaires. As the owner, you can do a personal letter with questions, create a comments blog on your website, or leave postage-paid questionnaires with customers. There are tons of ways to get feedback. The more you learn, the more you're able to fine-tune your customer experience.

My favorite customer experience story is about a dentist. He periodically sent out questionnaires to his patients and expected the usual complaints about the dental profession. But what he learned instead was that people wanted him to offer more flexible office hours—some wanted earlier times, other patients wanted him to be open later. He now opens the office at 5:30 a.m. on Tuesdays, closing at 3:30 p.m. On Thursdays, he opens at 11:00 a.m. and closes at 7:30 p.m. Patients love it, and he's enjoyed a nice bump up in business. The biggest downside? That old rhythm, routine, religion thing. After so many years of eight to five, he said it was hard to recalibrate his internal clock.

Every bit of feedback is important. I get stopped in the grocery store and people give me their opinions. I always listen and I always thank them. They're guiding me on how to be the business with which they want to do business.

PRODUCTS CREATE VIRAL OPPORTUNITY IF THE FIRST P AND E ARE IN LINE

The final P in PEP is, as you know, products. The mature business has probably used and/or offered the same products for a number of years. Twenty years ago, you might have been able to get away with that. You can't anymore. Improvements seem to happen daily. And if you're offering products that aren't current or forward thinking, customers may perceive you the same way—your "use by" date has expired.

I heard a story about a bakery that offered a few gluten-free products, but didn't promote this offering. Other bakeries were promoting gluten-free this and gluten-free that, capitalizing on the perception that gluten is bad for all of us. Now by my limited medical knowledge, gluten is only bad for if you have celiac disease, gluten sensitivity, or a wheat allergy. But I think because going gluten-free is such a health fad, and because this bakery didn't make known that it could accommodate those who'd embraced this craze—not to mention those who genuinely needed gluten-free items—many of their current and even potential customers' perceptions shifted negatively. Did it hurt the bakery's business? Hard to say. But several customers did mention it to the clerks working behind the counter (good customer feedback), and, based on those comments, the bakery put signs in the store window advertising their gluten-free menu.

The point is: stay current. Don't let real or imagined product deficiencies impact your customer's experience.

A mature traditional business that watches its PEP religiously should be able to stay level. I often refer to this as plateauing. This is a business that is operating at a certain level with only slight plus or minus variations. For many businesses, staying plateaued is what they want to do. They don't want to be bigger or better. They just want to remain the way they are. My problem with a plateaued company is, sooner or later, you know what's going to happen—it's going to reach the end of the plateau. It's going to plummet and fail.

Exercises:

☑ Run a PEP analysis on the state of the organization. Add one additional piece of information to the mix. Track your key financial indicators—gross sales, salaries, other expenses, debt, and profit—to see if in fact your "plateau" is level or if you're experiencing a slight climb or decline. This analysis may give you an indication of financial factors you can correct to stay "on the level."

☑ Create a customer questionnaire. What would you most like to learn from your customers? Figure out the best way to conduct your survey. Don't limit yourself to one format. Perhaps you can send a snail mail survey one quarter, and an e-survey the next.

☑ Create a space on your website for customer feedback. Customers have become comfortable doing this on sites like Amazon. By adding an opportunity for feedback, you'll not only look up to date, you'll gain valuable information. Make sure you monitor comments regularly, and don't let the space become an eyesore of negative information.

CHAPTER 10

WHERE DOES A MATURE COMPANY
FIND NEW GROWTH?

So what does a mature business do if it wants to escape the plateau and climb the growth curve instead of sliding down into decline? Figure 10.1 offers a sketch of possible directions for a mature company.

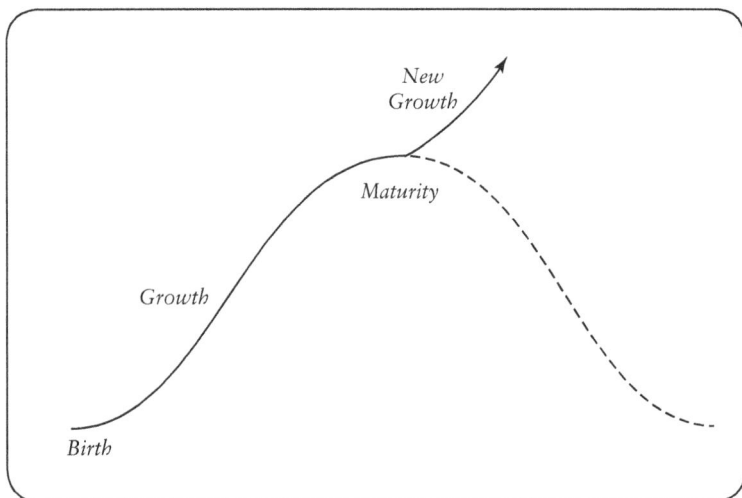

Figure 10.1 Finding the Path to New Growth

This is a subject I'm very passionate about because it's exactly what I faced with Apollo.

I'm not going to sugarcoat it—I found it incredibly hard and complex.

Why? Simple. It requires change. And change, well, that requires hard work. Change and hard work are two things mature traditional businesses don't like to do.

We've talked about the mature business getting in a rhythm, the rhythm becoming a routine, and the routine becoming a religion. Asking employees to change and work at something they don't perceive as their job is . . . heresy.

Your employees are going to look at you like you're worshipping pagan gods. Which in many ways is true—you're not operating the business for what it is *today*, you're operating for what you want it to be *tomorrow*.

When you start messing with the religion—it's just going to be you, pal.

Alone.

Employees will tell you they support you, but trust me, they're twirling a finger around their ears and saying to themselves, "You are crazy."

You have to stand straight and tall with confidence that the changes you're about to implement are what's best for the company. There will be times when you have inner doubts. Tune them out. There will be times when you want to quit. Push harder. There will be times when you need reassurance that there's a light at the end of the tunnel. That's what this book is for. I did it and I know you can, too. You're going to accomplish something that, at the end of your career, you can look back, smile, and say, "Yeah, I did that."

Growth is waiting. Let's get started.

THE $64 QUESTION: WHERE IS GROWTH GOING TO COME FROM?

There are a lot of different avenues open to you. All of which (well, most, anyway) are right answers. What I'm always searching for is the *right* right answer. Here's how we determined what that was at Apollo. Here's what we looked at.

Expanding Our HVAC Business Locally

- **Pros:** HVAC is our core business. We know it. We're good at it. We're staffed to accommodate growth.

- **Cons:** Crowded marketplace. Large spend to achieve incremental growth. No diversification from core business.

- **Possibilities:** Begin buying other HVAC firms and become the dominant company in our ADI (Area of Dominant Influence).

Expanding Our HVAC Business Regionally

- **Pros:** New markets present a big growth opportunity.

- **Cons:** Which markets? Must start from scratch building local customer base. High start-up cost. Difficulty of managing multiple locations.

- **Possibilities:** Buy an HVAC company out of market and use it as a base from which to build our business.

Offering HVAC Line Extensions

- **Pros:** Offers potential for larger tickets on jobs.

- **Cons:** We've already added some line extensions. The remaining ones don't generate enough volume to fuel growth. No diversification from core business.

- **Possibilities:** Search out the next "big" thing and add it to our lineup.

Adding a Complementary Business

- **Pros:** Would allow us to offer another service to our customers. Outside our core business so it would generate a separate revenue stream. Might offer relief from HVAC revenue seasonality.

- **Cons:** What complementary business? Will our customers use it? Lack of knowledge—don't even know what we don't know. Start-up costs.

- **Possibilities:** Hire an expert in that field; let him show us how to build the business.

Buying a Complementary Business

- **Pros:** Acquire more customers. Established revenue stream. Staff already in place.

- **Cons:** Which business to acquire? Cost. Cultural differences. Sunsetting of acquired management.

- **Possibilities:** Buy a smaller company so the cost isn't too great; use the acquisition as preparation for a larger acquisition.

Trying a Daffy, Harebrained Scheme (most we looked at are too idiotic to reveal)

- **Pros:** Like winning the lottery. Big bucks if you hit it.

- **Cons:** Not even a slim chance of success.

- **Possibilities:** Might cause you to stumble into something that would work.

+   +   +

At one time or another, we seriously—and by seriously I mean we spent time and money doing the due diligence—looked at each of these.

Let's take buying a complementary business as an example.

In our home market, there's a company with a name very similar to ours. We had discussions about buying the company. We didn't. We should have. It might have proven a good acquisition, but we never looked beyond that name to find out what kind of benefits it could have brought to Apollo. And so we didn't pull the trigger and buy it.

This is one of those cases where we were attracted to them for the wrong reason—they had that great name. We should have been selecting an acquisition target based on the company's customer base, their revenue stream, and their goodwill in the community. We weren't. We just liked that name.

Acquisitions is one of those areas where you shouldn't allow yourself to be attracted to any bright, shiny object. You have to be disciplined as to what you want, whom you talk to, and what you offer. Numbers are important. But again, this is a great time to look at PEP, because that's what you're really buying. Find a company with good PEP—people, experience, and product—and you'll make a smart acquisition.

The other thing that kept us from pulling the trigger on this one, as well as a number of other acquisitions and expansions we considered, was what psychiatrists call approach/avoidance reaction. Here's a relatable example of how this plays out.

It's time to buy a new car. I've decided to give up my

gas-guzzling SUV and go green. I've been reading everything I can about Tesla Motors and their electric cars. The model I'm interested in is the Model S. It's a four-door sedan that looks incredibly like an Aston Martin. I've built my car online, picked out the color, the interior, and the wheels. It is so perfect.

This is the "approach" part of the reaction. The more I think about my dream car the more excited I get.

I make an appointment to visit the showroom and order my Model S. The salesman greets me, we take an S for a test drive, and I am absolutely on cloud nine. Back in the show-room, the salesman presents the contract—it will take two months to custom-build my car—and goes over the deposit and financing plans.

Now, I knew how much this car was going to cost, so I'm not surprised at that.

But. But. But. Gulp. Decision time. Time to pull the trigger.

Suddenly my brain is going: *wait, wait, wait. Are you sure you want to do this? That's a lot of money. You'll have to wait two months for your car. It's electric—what if it breaks down?*

This is the "avoidance" part of the reaction. The closer you get to the point of decision, the more your mind shifts from approach (excitement) to avoidance (fear of commitment). Approach/avoidance is one of those facts of life. It affects commitments on marriage, home buying, pretty much everything—including making an important business decision.

The real reason we didn't acquire that well-named company is that we hit avoidance and couldn't get past that. This is where you have to have the courage to face your fears. If you've done your homework and made good decisions in your acquisition quest, those fears are nothing but head trash. Everybody has head trash. Smart CEOs/owners learn to ignore it. They *make* decisions. They don't avoid them or put them off.

Making the decision is the key. Once you're confident you can make the decision, it's time to shift your energies to making the right decision. How do you do that? Well, remember, whatever you decide to sell, your customers have to buy it. So why not involve them in the decision-making process?

At Apollo, we finally decided we wanted to *add* a complementary service. After much discussion, we narrowed it down to electric or plumbing, and we decided we'd rather grow the new line organically as opposed to buying an existing company.

So we emailed a questionnaire to our customers:

- If Apollo offered electric services, would you call us?

- If Apollo offered plumbing services, would you call us?

With each question, we asked for comments. What we learned was illuminating.

Customers told us they called an electrician about once every three years. Hmmm, not nearly as much potential as we expected. Customers also told us they called a plumber several times a year—and that those calls were for three very different things: clogged drains (this was the biggie); repairs to pipes, faucets, and fixtures; and dig jobs (like replacing a water line to the street). No pun intended, but plumbing had a much better revenue stream. And, of course, all this information was especially valid and valuable since it came from our own customers.

They pretty much made the decision for us. Plumbing it was.

Just one small issue . . . we didn't know diddly about plumbing. Not a speck. Kind of a daunting problem. So I studied it, soaked up everything I could, and guess what I discovered?

We were headed for another potential train wreck.

HVAC guys are techs. Plumbers are craftsmen. That's a huge difference. Plumbers have to have a license. HVAC techs aren't licensed—that doesn't mean they're any less proficient, but it does mean the two groups operate on different levels.

The more I studied plumbing, the more I realized I needed the insight of a licensed plumber to help me introduce this new service. I viewed this as hiring a consultant and began interviewing potential candidates.

If you've never done it, hiring a consultant is no more difficult than a staffing hire. By talking to a number of people, you gain a large-picture view of how they view the task and you learn their individual approaches. Both of these are valuable to learn.

I view this interviewing process as a chemistry test and would recommend you hire the consultant with whom you feel the most comfortable. Make sure this person is a fit for your organization as well. Above all, make absolutely sure you trust and respect the consultant, because you'll be using his or her advice to restructure your company.

It's easy to follow a consultant's recommendations when they agree with your own opinions and beliefs. But when you *disagree* with those recommendations, it's easier to listen and follow them when you have respect for the consultant. Remember, you're hiring her because she's the expert. Once she's on board, don't second guess or minimize her recommendations just because you don't agree with them.

In our case, the fellow we hired was a retired master plumber.

Truly knowledgeable. Likable. He sized up the task we'd given him and immediately began guiding us forward. Not everyone in the organization was as impressed with him as I was. This is to be expected. There's always grumbling when the new kid gets placed at the head of the line. The fact that you're paying attention to him creates uncertainty in the organization. That uncertainty feeds on itself and people start all sorts of crazy rumors. Best to keep everything you're doing transparent. You'll still get grumbling but not as much.

Our guy helped us set up the truck, order stock, and hire our first licensed plumber. He was just what we needed. But what if he hadn't been?

Finding out you've hired the wrong consultant can be frustrating. But don't let it cause you to lose faith in the direction you've set. If our guy hadn't worked out, I don't know if—at the time—I'd have had the courage to start the whole hiring process over. I might have given up or tried something else. In hindsight, that would have been a huge mistake. You have to have confidence in your vision, even if you make a few false steps at the beginning.

Again, with the 20/20 vision of hindsight, here's what I recommend you do at this early stage:

- **Put your plan on paper.** Think of it as creating a mini business plan. Once you have it written out, study it, see where it can be improved, and create second and third drafts. Keep refining until you feel it's exactly what you want. This document will serve as a compass, helping your efforts stay on course.

- **Make a succinct bullet-point version to hand out to employees.** Bullet points are best because employees are busy and no one likes to wade through tons of text. Bullet points also make sure employees understand the major points of your plan. By putting these major points in writing, you eliminate the possibility of employees hearing different things. What you don't want is employees talking among themselves, saying: "I heard this." "No, what I heard him say was this." and "You're both wrong; he said this." I call this the post-presentation death spiral. By the time they're finished, no one will have a clue what you really said.

- **Talk to key advisors outside the company.** Board members. Your CPA. Your attorney. Friends who are fellow business owners. They'll be a good test audience and they may add valuable insight to the plan. A caution: it's the job of advisors like CPAs and attorneys to warn you about all the pitfalls you may encounter. Listen to what they have to say, but turn it around—get their advice on how to preempt these trouble spots.

- **Consider getting your management team on board first.** Doing this says you value them. They'll be more inclined to support your plan if you share it with them privately and allow them to give input. Don't expect rousing support. Don't expect even lukewarm support. In most mature traditional businesses, these managers will be resistant to any change. Winning them over may take multiple meetings and considerable patience on your part. Remember, you are the adult in this relationship. The children will test you, as children do, to see how you react. Be understanding, but firm. It's your company, your plan, and you need to know who you can count on to help you achieve it. These meetings are early determiners of which managers stay and which you may need to replace. (If you have a manager that is particularly hostile, you may need to immediately terminate this person before continuing to move forward.)

- **Make your announcement an event.** When you're ready to share your plan with the entire company, don't call an impromptu meeting in the lunchroom. Hold it someplace that your employees will think is special. What you'd like is for your employees to equate the big-time announcement with the big-time surroundings. So don't skimp. Hold it off-site, cater in food, and allow enough time so your employees can soak it all in. Make sure everyone leaves with your bullet-point plan and possibly a memento of the event.

- **Don't hold a big announcement and then never follow up.** Plan periodically to give employees an update on the plan, to celebrate milestones, and to congratulate employees on their efforts in helping the plan succeed. Yes, you are the CEO/owner, but you need to be the head cheerleader, too.

✦   ✦   ✦

See the difference this kind of preparation can make by taking a look at the following two examples.

Steve's Announcement

I know a mature-business owner, Steve, who gathered his employees in the cafeteria and told them in glowing terms that he was going to revolutionize their industry. He was very vague on details, except that it would require all employees to work longer hours. He handed out a hastily put together employee handbook detailing what was expected. Steve finished his presentation to shock and silence. One by one, employees drifted into HR to ask what was going on. Unfortunately, HR didn't know either.

When Steve was asked later why he was so vague about his plan, he said he didn't want details to leak out to his competition. But that only made matters worse. Now his employees thought he didn't trust them. Needless to say, his plan quickly flopped.

Dan's Announcement

Dan, who had a similar industry-rattling plan for his business, handled things differently. He gathered his key managers at an off-site location, shared his plans in detail, and sought their input. He got plenty. Good and bad. Some he incorporated, some he didn't. He scheduled a second off-site, shared the revised plan, and asked each person if he had his or her support. Since they'd contributed to the plan, with the exception of one person, the plan had plenty of buy-in. Dan then scheduled a company-wide meeting. At that meeting, he shared his plan, the fact he'd gotten good input from the managers, and that they stood behind it. He finished by distributing a bullet-point overview of the plan and added that if anyone had questions or concerns he was happy to meet, listen, and discuss. Dan's thoughtful approach carried the day. Even the one manager who didn't initially support the plan came around.

Buy-in. It's all about feeling important and included. Dan did it. Steve stubbed his toe. So what do you need to do to be more like Dan, less like Steve?

THE FOUNTAIN OF YOUTH

Unlike the human life cycle, the business life cycle can be altered. The next phases for a mature business don't have to be decline and death. By adding a complementary service, a mature company can reverse the aging process and become more vibrant and vital. I call it the "fountain of youth" effect (see Figure 10.2).

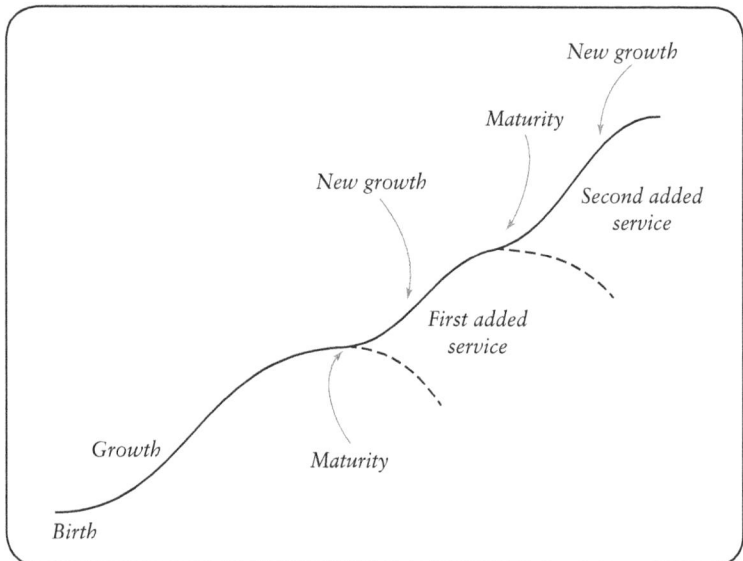

Figure 10.2 The Fountain of Youth

For Apollo, that fountain of youth began with plumbing. We were energized by adding a service that allowed us to expand and improve our customer relationship. Because when the customer relationship grows, it creates the opportunity for everything within the company to grow: revenue, staff, equipment, salaries. You've become a growth company again.

Essentially, what you've done is alter the bell curve. Instead of being at the top of the curve, plateaued, or beginning that downward path, you've kicked your business back into growth mode.

This is what visionary consumer businesses do all the time. The company that makes toothpaste begins offering mouthwash and toothbrushes. The company that makes lawn mowers begins offering snow blowers. The company that makes computers begins offering tablets and phones. They know that by providing expanded product and service offerings that make customers' lives easier, those customers will reward them with additional purchases.

These visionary businesses—many of them package-goods companies—have a finger on the pulse of their product offerings. The minute a product or service shifts into mature mode, the company is looking for a way—a line extension, a complementary product or service—to shift itself back into growth mode.

How do those CEOs/owners know what to do?

Simple. They talk to their customers. (Remember Apollo asking our customer base if we should add plumbing or electric?) By listening to their customers, visionary business leaders take some of the risk out of adding a new product or service. They know they have buy-in even before the product or service launches.

That's why we weren't surprised that plumbing was profitable from the get-go. Our initial plumbing hire was quickly joined by our second, third, fourth, and fifth. With each hire, our service offering became more robust and a more valued part of the company.

In fact, plumbing was such a success that we've now introduced a new offering: handyman services.

How did we come up with that? Again, we talked with our customers and found a real pent-up demand for someone reputable who could do small to medium-sized jobs in the home.

If Apollo's growth curve with the addition of plumbing was beginning to flatten out, handyman services will kick it back up.

That's the secret of the fountain of youth. Your company will stay eternally young if you continue to add and provide services that enhance your customer experience.

Exercises:

☑ Whiteboard your growth possibilities. What looks to have the most potential to benefit your company? Are you sure this is the *right* right answer? Early in the process is the time to involve advisors and benefit from their thoughts.

☑ Use your customers as a sounding board. Create a simple questionnaire to learn what additional service(s) or product(s) they'd like to see you offer.

☑ Visualize your preparation for an announcement. See yourself going through the steps to create an articulate strategy and presentation. Remember, you want to be like Dan, not Steve.

☑ How could your company be more nimble in responding to customer needs and wants? Is there a product or service that would give you a fuller, more complete customer relationship? If the answer is yes, good. What's stopping you from implementing it? If the answer is no, why not ask your customers what additional services they'd like you to provide?

CHAPTER 11

WITH GROWTH YOU NEED TO REBALANCE

When our newly hired Apollo plumber made his first service run, I felt a huge sense of accomplishment. Our complementary service line was up and running. It was definitely a high-five moment. But it was only a moment, because there was still plenty more that needed to be done.

That's because our company's infrastructure was designed for heating and cooling. Sure, we now had a personable plumber and a truck packed with plumbing parts. But we were missing systems to support that plumber.

Think of it this way—support systems are like the foundation of your home. When all the rooms of your home—living, dining, kitchen, bedrooms, garage—rest firmly on your home's foundation, things are in perfect alignment.

But what if you decided to add a family room? You think: *Great idea. The family would love it. More space. Hey, maybe get a 60-inch flat screen.* But would you build it without putting a foundation under it?

You could try to do it on the cheap and cantilever that room off the back of the house and it might—*might*—not break off and end up as a pile of expensive rubble on the back lawn. Or you could bite the bullet and pay the cost of putting in a foundation, knowing you'll be able to enjoy that space for years to come.

The same holds true for a business adding a new service. If you don't want that service to end up as the proverbial expensive pile of rubble, you have to give it the support of a solid foundation (see Figures 11.1 and 11.2).

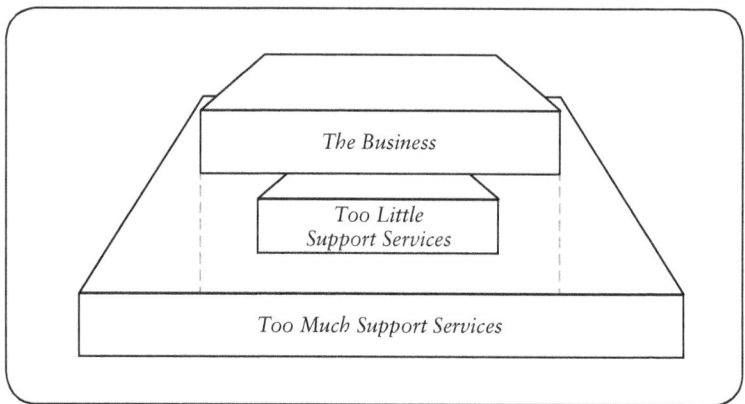

Figure 11.1 Sizing the Foundation

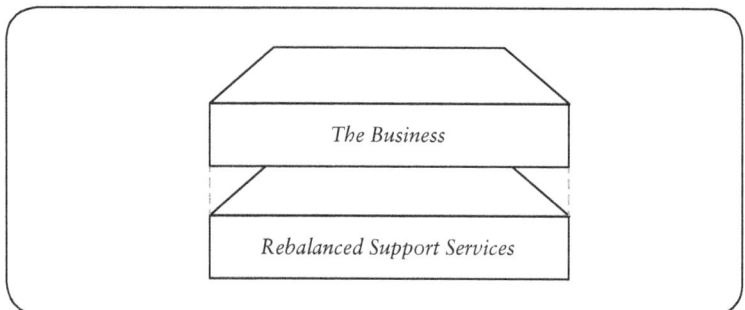

Figure 11.2 In Balance

Most businesses, however, want to launch new services as inexpensively as possible. So they don't invest in the foundation support systems needed to support the new service. They blissfully expect existing staff to take on the added work and somehow get everything accomplished.

This is almost dooming the new service to failure.

Traditional businesses, as a rule, have lean support systems. There's not much spare capacity. And the folks that staff these desks are by-the-rules people. They don't take kindly to having added responsibility dropped on their plates. In fact, they can be downright hostile.

LIGHTS ON, LIGHTS OUT

I heard the story of a lighting company (table lamps, floor lamps, chandeliers, outdoor lights) that wanted to add plumbing fixtures. The company did a good bit of business with homebuilders, and the idea was that builders could do one-stop shopping for lighting and plumbing fixtures. They ran the idea by a couple of their builders, who gave it a thumbs-up.

The store's owners, Shelly and Erin, hired a young lady, Britt, who had worked for a major plumbing supply house. Britt had all the contacts, knew what to order, and how to set up the in-store fixture displays. In six months' time, she had the plumbing side of the business up and running. Sales started slowly but picked up as builders, putting up market homes, were at the right point in the build to take advantage of the combined service.

Shelly and Erin were ecstatic.

Tim, the bookkeeper, was irate.

In addition to his normal work, he was now expected to deal

with all these new plumbing suppliers and handle all the additional accounts payable and accounts receivable. On multiple occasions Tim let Shelly and Erin know he was at his wit's end. He desperately needed help. They seemed oblivious.

Business would have continued that way—sales building, Shelly and Erin happy, Tim frazzled and grumpy—if it hadn't been for a change in Britt's life. She let Shelly and Erin know she and her husband were expecting their first child and she'd be out for three months on maternity leave.

Tim gleefully saw this as his opportunity to deep-six plumbing and return to his regular routine. As good/bad luck would have it, Tim shared an office with the HR person, Brenda. As office mates, Brenda and Tim had become friends, so when Tim suggested that Brenda drag her feet on hiring a replacement for Britt so that Tim could get a breather, she naturally said yes.

Tim saw the candidates Brenda was interviewing and suggested she hire Jason: a recent college grad (PR major) who knew nothing about plumbing fixtures but was desperate for a job. Brenda, caught up in employee health-care issues, liked—as Tim suggested—that Jason was a go-getter.

Britt's baby arrived early, so she was unable to train Jason. With no direction, Jason gamely met with the builders, who immediately recognized that deer in the headlights look—Jason didn't have a clue about what he was doing. Meanwhile, Tim was manipulating orders, payments, and deliveries to make Jason look bad. The combination proved to be too much. Orders arrived late; builders were overcharged; sinks came in the wrong sizes and showed up at the wrong job site.

The company's largest customer didn't say anything; he just

took his plumbing fixture business elsewhere. Other smaller builders did the same.

By the time Britt was ready to come back to work, Shelly and Erin had made the difficult decision that plumbing fixtures were no long viable and took the financial hit of shutting it down.

The blame fell on Jason. Plucky but incompetent.

Nobody ever suspected Tim, whose workload shrank back to what it had been before what was dubbed "the toilet fiasco" happened. Tim, age 61, retired on disability a year later.

So what did Shelly and Erin do right, wrong, and so-so?

Right:

- Shelly and Erin identified plumbing fixtures as a complementary service to lighting and queried their current clients as to whether they would use the service. With positive feedback, they moved forward.

- They recognized they needed someone with plumbing fixture experience to oversee this new service offering. After interviewing multiple candidates, they selected Britt and gave her the authority to make the new service offering a reality.

- Shelly and Erin never second-guessed Britt. Neither did they skimp on anything she asked for.

So-so:

- Shelly did bring all the employees together to introduce Britt and let everyone know the company was embarking on an exciting new venture. Unfortunately, Erin never explained how the new service would benefit the employees, nor did she seek buy-in from the group.

Wrong:

- Erin, who was COO, never thought about support services. She was totally concentrated on what was happening in the showroom.

- Shelly and Erin's biggest lapse in planning may have been in not identifying who would shoulder the back office work to make plumbing fixtures a success. If they had, they would have seen that the bulk of that work would fall on Tim's shoulders. Because they weren't aware of Tim's extra burden, they couldn't pro-actively address it. When Tim tried to talk to them, they were not responsive.

This last point, to me, was the tipping point between success and failure.

When a company adds a major new service offering, as Shelly and Erin did with plumbing fixtures or as Apollo did with plumbing, all support services—facilities, accounting, marketing, HR—need to be looked at and rebalanced.

Rebalanced? Do you wonder what that means?

It goes back to the foundation (support services) on which the business rests. How must support services change in order to support current activity? In Shelly and Erin's case, they should have seen that accounting would become overloaded and taken steps to add a junior person to support Tim. There may have been other rebalancing needed, too, but Tim's situation should have been obvious.

Had Shelly and Erin looked strategically at rebalancing support services, they would have realized Tim was a sleeper zombie.

Sleeper zombie?

Yep. Sleeper zombies are individuals who just need a trigger—an event, a slight, an overload—to be activated.

In Tim's case, all the ingredients were lurking below the surface waiting to be triggered. Let's take a look at them: Tim worked his entire career in a regimented part (accounting) of a traditional business. He viewed the company's path much as he viewed accounting principles—there were accepted practices, and one didn't deviate from those accepted practices. The idea of change was as foreign to him as the idea of wearing two left shoes.

Tim was 61 years old and well into retiring on the job. He was at a point in his career where he had no desire to learn something new, work overtime, or help the company build for the future. He just wanted to putter at his desk, banter with Brenda, and finish out his time.

The plumbing fixture business represented everything Tim didn't want. It was change—it took him out of his comfort zone. It was new—and because it was new and everything was untried, there was the opportunity for failure, and the last thing Tim wanted at the end of his career was failure. And it was physically more work. To a man who was winding down, it was like moving the finish line forward in a race. He wasn't sure he could make it.

Any or all of those things could have been the trigger. Tim, now an activated zombie, didn't think he was wrecking the company; he was only trying to keep his comfortable world from spinning out of control.

Exercises:

☑ If you were to add a complementary service line, what support services would you need to rebalance to support it?

☑ Looking at your organizational chart of 3-by-5-inch cards, do you have the right people in the right places to enable an additional service line to be successful?

☑ Do you see zombies or do you have sleeper zombies that should be dealt with?

CHAPTER 12

WHO'S WITH YOU, AND WHO'S NOT

Okay, let's review here: As the CEO/owner of a traditional business, you know that adding a complementary service will diversify and strengthen your maturing business, moving your company back into growth mode. You've researched services, run them by your customers, selected the most promising idea, brought in someone to get you started, and (unlike Shelly and Erin) you've rebalanced your support services.

Job well done, right? You can put the business on autopilot.

No. No. No. No. No.

This isn't the movie *Groundhog Day*. You're no longer a company that has the same year, year after year after year. You've instituted change into the equation and change needs to be managed by the big guy at the top—yeah, you.

Fortunately, you have a valuable tool to help you. That PEP analysis we talked about earlier is going to be your dashboard. It will serve you well in navigating the perils ahead.

I found, and I think you'll find too, that institutional change is incredibly difficult. It offers huge rewards—in terms of income, job satisfaction, and accomplishment—but that old saying is so, so true: *Good things don't come easy.*

Your PEP analysis will help tilt the odds in your favor. Let's look at your first P tool—that organization chart of 3-by-5-inch cards. These are the people who will carry the company forward . . . or hold it back.

In my earlier book, *Squirrels, Boats, and Thoroughbreds,* I talked about "pull theory." It's worth revisiting that for a moment. Pull theory contends there are two types of business environments—push and pull.

In the *push environment,* which is prevalent in most traditional businesses, the CEO/owner has to constantly push the employees for better results. Much of this has to do with traditional-business employees being hourly. Many hourly employees—not all—are focused on putting in their forty hours and not making more work for themselves. It's a "me versus the company" scenario that truly benefits neither.

In the *pull environment,* employees pull the company forward, because they are incentivized for the results they generate. In this scenario, the employee benefits by having the opportunity to earn more during his or her forty-hour week, and the company benefits from the cumulative increase in results.

There's another reason to move from push to pull: your sanity. As CEO/owner, pushing five people is very doable. But what if the business grows to twenty? Sixty? A hundred? You can't do it. But if a pull company grows from five to twenty to sixty to a hundred, the force keeps getting stronger.

On your P organization chart, look at each person. Is he or she someone you have to push? Or is this person someone who has the ability to pull the company forward? Here are a few clues to determine in which category your employee fits:

- **Push employees will see a new initiative as a threat.** They'll do whatever is within their means to maintain the status quo. If that means sabotaging a new service offering, well, too bad for you, the CEO/owner.

- **Pull employees will welcome a new initiative, seeing it as an opportunity** to increase income and/or rise further in the organization. They'll grab the ball and run with it.

So, looking at your organizational chart, here are the things you want to determine:

- Is this a push or pull employee? If he or she is a push employee, is the motivation there for that person to become a pull employee?

- Where is each employee in his or her personal life cycle? Are there people close to retirement or who have retired on the job who won't buy in to support the new service offering?

- Are there additional positions that need to be added to give the new service offering a solid foundation of support services? If so, what are the dynamics of adding those new individuals into the mix?

We're spending this time with the organization chart to get a sense of who's with us and who—potentially—is against us. What you don't want are naysayers who will undermine your effort to launch a new service offering. All it takes is one zombie to infect the organization and diminish your chances for success.

So put on your zombie-hunter hat and go over that organization chart with a fine-tooth comb. Zombies you should spot easily. Sleeper zombies are harder to spot but will make themselves evident as the new service launches.

Your goal is to take action against potential zombies. That can take several forms:

- You can put that person on a work program or, if you already have cause, dismiss him or her.

- You can do a rebalance and neutralize this person's ability to cause harm.

- You can move this individual into a position where he or she can't do any harm.

All three are workable solutions. Long term, you'll want employees who are pulling the company forward. So if you choose the option of sidelining or neutralizing problem individuals, know you've just kicked the can of dealing with them down the road.

My recommendation would be to do a rebalance and eliminate as many push employees as you can, as quickly as you can. Free of people dragging their heels, you may be surprised by the pickup in organizational momentum.

Don't view this rebalance as a one and done. You may move individuals with potential into more important roles. Bring in outside talent. Shuffle departments. Create an executive management group. All of these approaches are good and should make your company and your efforts better.

Just remain vigilant. Your new management group, as an example, may jell and be more than you expected. Or you may find that, after a year, one person just isn't a fit.

Don't be afraid to rebalance again. And if something else causes concern, don't be afraid to rebalance yet again. In this regard, you're like the general manager of an NFL team. The GM has starters and backups at every position and is always looking to put his most productive group on the field.

But you know what? Injuries happen. Chemistry changes. In the NFL, if there's no chemistry between the highly paid wide receiver and the super highly paid quarterback, one of them (chances are good it's the one who makes less) is going to go. For a GM, it's a mindset of constant review and improvement.

That's the way you need to look at your P organization chart: constant review and improvement.

Exercises:

☑ Is your organization push or pull? If push, how entrenched is this in the organization? What would it take to shift into a pull mode? Do you have the time and resources to make this a priority? Do you have the time to shift from push to pull prior to launching a complementary service?

☑ Looking at your P organizational chart, what changes are needed to: Move from push to pull? Eliminate zombies and sleeper zombies? Provide a solid foundation of support services for a new initiative?

☑ How would a rebalance help your company? Do a projected rebalance and then list all the benefits to the company. Do this from the employees' standpoint so that you can share this with them and develop buy-in to the rebalance.

CHAPTER 13

ARE YOU EXPERIENCED?

I saw a great sign on the wall in a company's lunchroom. It said: NO CUSTOMERS, NO COMPANY.

How true. How true.

Which brings us to the E in PEP—your customer experience.

Nothing, repeat nothing, will make a new offering fail faster than a bad customer experience—which is why it bears another look in this chapter.

In today's connected world, buzz—good or bad—spreads like wildfire. How fast is that, you ask? Here's how fast something bad can happen.

A guy I knew was into craft beer. He loved the brewing process, the different tastes, the crazy names. He reveled in the lore of craft brewing. Wasn't long before he was experimenting with different recipes in his basement. He'd make a small batch of this, small batch of that, and invite friends over for a tasting. I was one of those friends. It was always a fun time and I thought some of his beers were the equals of any on the market.

Well, he tinkered with his recipes and he finally created what he referred to as "the one." I tasted it and let me tell you, it was superb. Gaining confidence from the compliment, he entered it into a craft beer festival. Where he also received good—not stellar—but solid reviews. With that encouragement, he thought he could make it in the craft brewing business and he proceeded to drop a chunk of change on taking his craft beer to the market.

The day it was officially for sale, he had a launch party. Twenty-four hours later, he was washed up.

A respected local blogger on craft beers wrote: "I wonder which horse it came from?" That was all it took, that one negative comment. My friend's beer never overcame the bad buzz. Now, he's as bitter as bad beer.

No customers. No company.

So as you think about launching a complementary service, it's important that you exercise your E and look at every aspect of the new service from the customer's point of view.

Apollo is doing this now with our new handyman services offering. I mentioned earlier that we regularly do customer surveys. When queried about handyman services, the customer response was always positive. Buoyed by that, we began looking for a "prototypical" handyman. Or it could have been handywoman. As it turned out, it was a guy.

He was one of those people who seemed intuitively to know how to fix anything, could do fine finish work, and was a true people person.

One of the things we learned from talking with our customers was that they were looking for us to vet these handymen and send only responsible, safe people on calls to customers' homes. We do that. We're very diligent in checking the background, work, and work ethic of every technician we employ.

Even with that, when that individual shows up at the customer's home for the first time, that customer is wary. A ready smile and a friendly manner go a long way to putting a customer at ease. An ability to explain what he's about to do helps, too.

As with any business, the really good people are hard to get. My advice: don't settle until you find someone with all the attributes you're looking for. We looked at a lot of people before we found the guy we wanted. He was personable, professional, and proactive. I wouldn't have to push him; I knew he'd pull handyman services forward.

Before we hired him, however, I asked myself: *How will customers relate to him?* Everyone has pluses and minuses—there's no Superman out there—but I thought this fellow had the skills to be exceptional.

We gave him a solid understanding of Apollo and how we do business before he had his first customer appointment.

Despite the fact I thought he was exceptional at the job, I contacted customers after each of his appointments to get their opinion of his time in their home and learn if they were satisfied with the results.

I'm pleased to report the customer comments were overwhelmingly positive. The one area of concern was cost. Most customers had no idea what's involved in, say, hanging a door, or what the cost should be. Our policy was to provide a written estimate up front. But we learned that things—like hanging a door—needed a little more explanation before they got the estimate so the customer had context for those costs. We immediately put that into practice.

Sad to say, but many consumers have had bad experiences with tradespeople. Your company ends up being tarred with that same brush. So you have to work even harder to overcome distrust.

We also followed up with customers two months later to make sure they were still pleased with our work. If they say yes, the phone call often generates new business. If they aren't, you have the opportunity to win them over a second time.

Win them over? Are you crazy?

I'm sure many people think it is crazy, but I'm right about this. Your biggest opportunity comes from a negative. People don't expect you to make good on your work. So when you do, when you go out of your way to make it right, they often reward you with new business.

I saw this play out big time out on my street. One of my neighbors had her driveway blacktopped. She contracted with a good company. They arrived on time, completed the job in a professional manner. Just one problem. Halfway through the job, it began to rain. No, rain doesn't do this justice. It flat-out poured for half an hour. Then the sun popped back out. She came home to find a driveway that, because of the rain, had swirls where the old driveway showed through. She immediately called the coating company.

Here's where it gets interesting. You would expect the owner of the company to have good customer service skills. But how about the receptionist who took my neighbor's call?

Is she going to be hostile because you've pulled her away from a task she's trying to finish? Is she going give the customer the runaround: *You'll have to talk to so and so. He's not in right now. Do you want his voicemail?* Or even worse: *That's an act of God. We're not responsible.*

Thankfully, in this case, the receptionist listened to my neighbor and immediately apologized on behalf of the company: "I am so sorry. We'll get a crew there immediately and recoat."

An hour later, they were working on her driveway. Did a beautiful job. No more swirls. Just a uniformly even jet black. She was pleased. I know this whole story because she was so pleased with the way she was treated that she told it to me when she recommended them.

Now, every new service has some stumbles. We had them when we launched plumbing. I'm sure we'll have a few with handyman services. If you view them as opportunities instead of problems, it will make you a stronger, more responsive customer-oriented company.

Making the job right might cost you your profit for that particular job. You may even lose a little money. No businessperson likes that to happen, but let me tell you the upside: You send a message to the organization that anything less than a professional job simply isn't acceptable. A lot of companies say that, but don't put their money where their mouth is. Those companies that do seem to have fewer problems. It's as if employees know they're held accountable to a higher standard.

ONE FINAL E SUGGESTION KAIZEN AND THE NEW CUSTOMER EXPERIENCE

Earlier, we talked about *kaizen*, the continuous improvement process used by companies like Toyota to find inefficiencies. Before you launch your new service, I'd recommend you do what I'm going to call an E *kaizen*.

Look at each step in your process from the customer's point of view and see where you might be able to make the experience better. Chances are good you'll find things that can be made more customer friendly with a little tweaking. Even if you don't, walking in your customer's shoes will give you insights into how to best communicate your new service in a way that resonates with customers.

Exercises:

☑ Looking at your new service from the consumer's point of view, do you have the right people in the right roles? Do you have capacity or are you spread too thin?

☑ Use your whiteboard to do an E with *kaizen*. Start by creating a schematic of each step in the process and how it affects the customer relationship. Do you see improvements that will make the customer relationship better?

☑ Create a plan for stumbles. If something happens—who will deal with it? How will it be resolved? What will you do to keep it from happening again?

☑ Look for ways to create good buzz. Twitter, YouTube, Facebook—whatever you're comfortable doing, use it to generate good word of mouth.

CHAPTER 14

STANDING OUT

The third part of our PEP analysis is the P for product. Since many of you will be value-added resellers (we'll get to services in a moment), you may think this P stands for *punt* because the manufacturer—not you—controls the product.

I'm going to suggest that P—rather than product—actually stands for *perception.*

Again, let's use Apollo as an example. We sell two quality furnace lines. Neither manufacturer lets us spec the furnaces they make for us. They're made to factory spec and other resellers have the same furnaces we do.

So if you look at things narrowly, we offer an undifferentiated product. That would be a problem if the customer were buying only the furnace. But I believe customers buy furnaces in the larger sense—they view the product as the furnace *and* the installation.

That's why you can think of the product P as *perception*. It's how the customer *sees* the product. In this case, having the customer view the product in the larger sense allows us to shift from selling an undifferentiated product to a differentiated one. We add differentiation in the installation. We talk about the hundred hours of training our techs receive each year and the experience they've gained in tackling tough furnace installs. So the product we sell is the equipment, sure, but it's also our knowledge and experience installing that equipment.

Differentiation gives the customer a reason to choose Apollo over other suppliers. It will give them a reason to choose you, too.

Your new service offering may involve an undifferentiated product. If it does and you don't differentiate it, if you don't try to make it stand out in some way, you'll likely blend in with the pack, giving the customer no clear reason to choose you.

Standing out through differentiation is the way you catch the customer's eye. If you blend in, you won't be seen.

I heard the story of a small advertising agency whose offices were hidden away in a four-story office building. It was the old problem: out of sight, out of mind. The principals decided they needed more exposure and bought a two-story frame house on a commercial street. Their new quarters had their name on a sign above the front door, and they enjoyed better visibility than they'd had in the office park. Still, they weren't getting as much differentiation and visibility as they wanted.

Until they painted the building an eye-popping bright yellow.

On a street of red brick and brown and gray frame houses, they definitely stood out. They leveraged it with yellow briefcases and business cards. Suddenly, they were the ad guys everyone was talking about. Their business boomed. All because they had a good idea about standing out.

Don't view your product as just product. View it through the lens of perception and see if you can differentiate it in a way that makes you more appealing to your customers.

Now let's talk about the P for an added service. This is where those guys who work in the yellow building excel. It's called branding. And what branding does for you is create the differentiation of a unique service personality.

Remember Mr. Goodwrench?

How about the Maytag repairman?

Or the GEICO gecko?

Personalizing the service helps customers relate and remember your new service. I mention personalization because it often creates the ultimate branded service. But there are many other ways to brand. For example, there's a bank that offers "Five-Star Service," a car dealer who offers "Signature Service," even a car wash that calls its top wash "The Works."

Don't be afraid to come up with something outrageous. The more you stand out, the better. The way you judge whether what you've come up with is what you want to use is by viewing it from your customer's perspective. If it plays with them, it's going to be good for you.

I mean, who wouldn't want "The Works" car wash, or "Signature Service" at the dealership, or "Five-Star Service" at the bank?

This second P may be the trickiest to understand and implement, but if you do it right, boy, does it pay off with results.

Exercises:

☑ What can you do to make an undifferentiated product your own? Will the manufacturer allow private branding? (An example of private branding would be if our furnace supplier allowed us to pair their logo with Apollo's. Many big chains like Sears sell a number of privately branded products. For years, Michelin made tires that Sears sold under the Sears name.) If private branding isn't a possibility, will the manufacturer make a special run for you that would make your products different in some way?

☑ What can you bundle with your undifferentiated product to differentiate it? People? Service? Location? Look for things that will allow you to stand out to customers.

☑ In your market, pay attention to who has branded service. Look at things from the consumer's perspective. Who has done a good job and who hasn't? Why? Understanding the answers to these questions will help you be successful.

☑ Try your hand at branding a service offering. Come up with several ideas that you can measure against each other to see which one is the best. Not good at this kind of right-brain stuff? Find the guys in the yellow house in your town. Hire them to come up with some options for you. Tell them you want something wonderful that helps you stand out. Get their recommendations on which option they think will work best, but then—go with your gut. It's your business. You'll need to embrace this and live with it for, like, forever.

CHAPTER 15

REVERSING THE FORTUNES OF A DECLINING BUSINESS

I know you may not want to do it, but if you're a traditional business in decline, you need to think of your company as a patient being wheeled into the emergency room. You're there because the company is hemorrhaging money and you can't get the red ink to stop. Doctors and nurses are running alongside the gurney, desperately watching the company's vital signs and trying to diagnose what's causing the hemorrhaging.

That red ink you're bleeding is only a symptom. They're racing against the clock to figure out what's wrong with the company and how to best treat it.

BUYING TIME

To stanch the bleeding, one of the emergency room's first actions will be to start an IV and administer fluids. And for you, an influx of new capital will buy time to finish the diagnosis and begin treatment. Like a rare blood type, that new capital can be hard to come by. Your line of credit may be tapped out. Credit cards, too. Is it hopeless? You have to ask yourself: *How important is saving this business?* Is it important enough to borrow from family? Take a second mortgage on the house? Raid your 401(k)? Only you can make that decision. Use your head, but listen to your heart.

WHAT'S WRONG?

Your mature business was feeling just fine and then it started experiencing problems. Here's what the docs might be looking for:

- **Obesity:** The management ranks have grown too fat and the payroll too large for the company's size.

- **Bad DNA:** If yours is a family business, it could be affected by family infighting or family members who aren't pulling their weight.

- **Low blood pressure:** If key staffers have left, the company might not have the juice to get its work done. Stand up quickly and you're suddenly lightheaded.

- **Dementia:** Your product or service is no longer in demand, so your sales and revenue have fallen. Or it could be that the population with a need for your product has shifted away from you.

- **Poor self-esteem:** Outside competition has moved into the market. Sad to say, the new kid in school has bloodied your nose and taken your lunch money.

- **Job-related injuries:** For a value-added reseller, product changes by the manufacturer may have weakened the relationship you have with your customers. Worse, a product recall might ruin that relationship altogether.

- **Concussion:** You were the victim of bad buzz. Competitors did a number on your head.

- **Catastrophic injury:** BOOM. You were hit with a fire, a flood, or some other natural disaster.

THE DANGER OF SELF-DIAGNOSIS

Sometimes traditional companies in decline can be objective and self-diagnose their problem. Most times, however, they are too close to it to see things objectively. In these cases, companies seldom deal with the real problem or problems, but pick something—a scapegoat—that they can "fix" to make the problems go away.

There was a small nursery business, located in one of a city's inner suburbs that had fallen into decline. The business was owned by a husband and wife in their 60s and run by their son who was in his 30s. The nursery, which wasn't doing well, had a particularly poor spring and a family meeting was called. Mom, Dad, and Son sat at the kitchen table and tried to figure out what the problem might be. The son told his parents: "It's got to be my fault. I wasn't working hard enough. I wasn't getting everybody else to work hard enough." The parents immediately came to his rescue and said: "No, it was our fault. We spent too much time this winter in Arizona." Both vowed to do better. Unfortunately spring was over; there was no redo on their big selling season. They toughed out the rest of the year by going deeper into their line of credit and hoped next year's spring would be better.

It wasn't.

Neither Mom and Dad nor Son had been the problem. They were the victims of population shift. The new home market had shifted to the outer suburbs. That's where folks were buying trees and putting in shrubs. New nurseries had sprung up in these outer suburbs. Why would a gardening enthusiast drive past one of those new nurseries to go to Mom and Dad's?

Faced with bankruptcy, Mom and Dad sold the place to a competitor for half of what it was worth. Had they brought in an outside business consultant, he might have told them to buy a piece of ground in the outer suburbs and put in a satellite store with the objective of shifting the business and, eventually, making that their main location. Would that have saved their business? Hard to say. But it would have given them a better chance at survival. Often, when you're fixing the wrong problem, the real problem gets worse. In this case, you're your own worst enemy.

LISTEN TO THE DOCTOR

A security company that provided private security for businesses, public venues (racetracks, fairs, sporting events), and private homes was sinking deeper and deeper into red ink. They'd had three unprofitable years in a row, each one worse than the one before. Management wasn't paying attention and it was the company's banker, Mark, who sounded the alarm.

Mell was the firm's CEO/owner. A former policeman who had retired on disability from the force, Mell built the business by hiring other former policemen who had been friends. He'd also brought his two sons, Lance and Aaron, into the business and hoped to sell it to them in a few years to fund his retirement.

Mark introduced Mell to an accountant, Gary. Mark thought Gary could get Mell's business back on track. Gary went over the books, spent time in the offices, and met with Mell's sons and others in the organization. It didn't take him long to see the problem.

Mell had made both his sons and six of his friends supervisors. Each of them was making supervisor's money, but only three of them were doing supervisor's work. Although Gary would never have explained it this way—Mell had five zombies feeding on his organization.

Mell's older son, Lance, seldom came into the office and when he was there he spent most of his time drinking coffee and laughing it up with the guys in the squad room. Jim, Ken, Robert, and Peter (the policeman friends) did a few supervisory checks but mostly hid behind their desks. The cumulative effect was five salaries with little benefit to the company.

When Gary made his recommendations to Mell—establish a work plan for Lance and eliminate the four cronies—Mell didn't want to hear it. He stormed around the conference room, shouting, yelling, and blamed poor bookkeeping for the firm's troubles. He was so obstinate that Gary had to reinvolve Mark to lay down the law: "Make the recommended changes, or the bank's calling your note."

Mell, grumbling and whining, conceded to Gary's recommendations and, with the zombie issues resolved, the company found its way back to profitability.

Sometimes the medicine doesn't taste good. Prepare yourself for that.

THE ZOMBIE FACTOR

Mell had two different types of zombies in his organization.

Lance thought he was owed a big salary because he was Mell's son. You hear that and you just want to knock some sense into this kid. His father was trying to do something good for his sons and Lance paid him back with ingratitude.

The cronies were even worse. They preyed on Mell's friendship for executive positions with wildly overblown salaries and conspired behind his back to keep him from realizing how little they did.

So on our list of illnesses, zombies caused Mell's business to suffer from obesity and bad DNA. Make no mistake, zombies can be the catalyst in low blood pressure, concussion, and catastrophic injury, as well.

The traditional business in decline needs every employee pulling the company forward to help it return to profitability; it can't afford to harbor even one zombie.

In Mell's case, he was too close to the problem to see it. These were friends and family. If, like Mell, you're too close to the situation, then you need a Gary to objectively look at the organization, see who can be saved and who has to go.

Don't hesitate. Hire the best person you can find. And don't even think about second-guessing him or her.

Exercises:

☑ Do you have a financial resource you could call on in an emergency? Wouldn't it make sense to set one up? Even if you never use it, you'd have the comfort of knowing it's there.

☑ Use each of these potential illnesses as a diagnostic. Do you see signs that one or more of them are already present in the organization? Do you see signs that one or more of them could develop within the organization?

- **Obesity:** How fat are your management ranks? Is your payroll too large for the company's size?

- **Bad DNA:** Are you a family business? If you answered yes, is there family infighting or family members who aren't pulling their weight?

- **Low blood pressure:** Have you lost key staffers? Is it difficult to get work accomplished on time? Are you falling further and further behind? What do you need to do to catch up? How quickly can you make that happen?

- **Dementia:** Is your product or service an anachronism? Has the market for your product moved away from you? How fast is demand falling? What has replaced you?

- **Poor self-esteem:** Just how tough is that outside completion? What's it going to take to get your lunch money back? What are their weaknesses? How can you exploit them?

- **Job-related injuries:** Has the manufacturer changed the product, and are your customers saying they liked the old one better? What can you do about that? Change manufacturers? Do something extra for your customers?

- **Concussion:** Ouch, you suffered a bad case of the bad buzz. What are you doing to counteract that? What good buzz can you get out into the marketplace? Who can you get to help you buff up your image?

- **Catastrophic injury:** Noah handled the flood. You, too, can survive a catastrophe, but you can't do it without a plan. Do you have a disaster plan? A recovery plan? Better yet, what systems can you put in place to keep a disaster from happening?

☑ If you needed an outside consultant to help you diagnose the symptoms and treat the illness, who would you use? Do you have an accountant or lawyer who might perform this function? Better yet, is there someone who could serve on your board and be of service year-round?

CHAPTER 16

BLOOD WORK

Doctors use blood work to get a measure of how a patient's body is functioning. White blood cells may be high. Lipid profile out of whack. Albumin low. Whatever is going on, the blood work numbers tell the story.

The same is true for your financials. Most traditional businesses in decline didn't just drop off a cliff and plummet straight down to the black hole of bankruptcy. Decline happens over a period of months, sometimes even years. And by carefully reviewing your financials, the numbers will tell you the story.

This might be a job for you and your accountant. Look for changes in revenue streams. For example, at Apollo, HVAC service, new installations, and plumbing are separate revenue streams. If new installations, as an example, were trending down over a period of months, I'd be looking for the reasons why:

- Was a competitor getting that business?

- Were we not recommending new installations to customers?

- Was there something wrong with our new installation team?

The numbers tell you the problem area. Then it's up to you to figure out what's causing it. The diagnostic tool I'd use first is the PEP analysis. Once the blood work has identified the problem, can you tell whether it was caused by one PEP factor or by a factor combination?

PEP ANALYSIS

People

- Is this a people-related problem? Are our people making customers think we don't like to do new installs? Are our installers part of the problem?

Experience of Customers

- Is there bad buzz about our installations? Are we messy? Slow? Has a competitor wowed customers and changed expectations?

Product

- Do customers not like the furnaces we offer? Is there a new product on the market that's making what we carry outdated?

So which part of PEP is at fault? Most times it isn't as easy as identifying one thing. It will be a combination of things that require initiatives in several areas. In our hypothetical install example, the combination could be that (1) customers don't like the brands we carry and because of that, (2) our staff has backed off recommending new installs. Although the first reason is clearly more important than the second, both need to be addressed to solve the problem.

PREP FOR SURGERY

Our earlier examples of businesses in decline assumed there was sufficient runway to resolve problems. Returning to our medical analogy, our patients were prescribed courses of medicine and were expected to recover.

But what if the blood work shows the company only has thirty days before it bleeds out? What if there isn't time or medicine to keep the company alive?

If things are moving this quickly, brace yourself; surgery may be needed. After all, better to lose an arm or a leg than your life.

THE GIANT CLIENT

Rick was a graphic designer who found a niche doing web pages and interactive brochures. He started this business in a spare bedroom and, in fourteen months, had sufficient work to move out of the spare bedroom to a business complex of small office suites. He also added his first employee, Ben, a computer programmer.

Two years later, Rick made Ben a partner. Rick owned 65 percent of the company, Ben 35 percent.

Fast-forward five more years. Rick and Ben (now in much larger digs) had one giant client, six smaller clients, and sixteen full-time and three part-time employees. The business was profitable. Rick and Ben's partnership was solid. Buzz on the street was good.

In fact, they had just presented a new website to the giant client and the client left beaming. The presentation went so well, that evening Rick and Ben hosted a happy hour for the staff to thank them for all their hard work.

The next morning Rick got an email—that's right, an email—saying the client had decided to go with another "vendor" and that the new vendor would not only be doing the new website but also all the company's other work too.

Rick and Ben tried to get a meeting with the client to learn what had soured the relationship but all requests were refused. Two weeks later, Ben bumped into one of the client's senior managers at a school function (both had children in the third grade). The manager confided to Ben that the company's president had a nephew, Todd, with a design business, and the work had been given to him. To add insult to injury, Todd hadn't even made a presentation. This was nepotism at its worst.

Without the giant client, Rick and Ben's business would implode. The six small clients didn't combine for enough income to continue Rick and Ben's current business configuration.

The two partners had known for a long time that having one client that dominated the shop could cause havoc. But they were determined not to let the loss of that client doom their business.

They knew the only way to stay in business was to cut staff. And cut deep. Two days after they received that email from the client, they met individually with each member of the staff. Each staffer was given two weeks severance and a letter of recommendation. By the time the day was done, the company was just Rick and Ben again.

Hard as it was to lose staff that felt like extended family, the two partners knew the income from the six small clients was only enough to cover the two of them and fixed expenses. By cutting the staff, Rick and Ben weren't hoping some miracle would bail them out, and they weren't willing to go into debt waiting for that to happen. They realistically scaled the business's expenses to keep them in line with income. Both partners thought if they could stabilize the business, they could find other clients and rebuild.

Granted, surgery like that—losing the entire staff—isn't something you want to do. But Rick and Ben were smart enough to realize it was the only way to keep their business from falling down the rabbit hole.

Eban, discussed next, was forced to take even more aggressive action.

ARM AND A LEG

Eban owned and operated a dry cleaning business that he ran from a small storefront in a well-trafficked shopping center. Eban had an assistant, Wanda, who had worked in the shop for fifteen years. Eban's wife, Helena, handled the office part of the business and their three teenage daughters also helped out in the store, giving relief to Wanda.

If you asked Eban how his 25-year-old business was doing, he'd tell you: "Fine." But in truth, it was dying slowly. After year five, each year for Eban was down from the last, even though Eban's customer service was superb.

Eban knew what was affecting his business. He considered "casual Fridays" the devil's work. As workplace dress had become more casual and common, his business had suffered. Eban knew there was no getting this genie back in the bottle. Business suits and dress shirts were as out of date as Roman togas.

Eban, however, had a plan. The storefront next to his—a pet supply store going out of business because it couldn't compete with the big-box stores—was about to be available. Eban snatched up the lease with the idea of enlarging his space. His thinking was that with a larger shop he could handle more volume and generate more revenue.

At the family dinner table, his oldest daughter, Iris, proposed another idea. Iris had a small home business designing note cards using rubber stamps and colored inks. She bought her rubber stamps online and was convinced that if there was a store that specialized in rubber-stamping supplies, stamping enthusiasts would flock to it. "Why not," she asked her father, "open that store in the new space?"

Eban was horrified. He crossed his arms. His mind was set. No. Stamp art was a nice hobby and Iris had made a little money at it, but a business?

Helena came to her daughter's rescue. "What would it hurt to try it for a couple of months?" she asked. "If it works, wonderful. If it doesn't, you have the space to enlarge the shop."

The battle raged for three days, mostly for Eban to save face.

Helena was the business brains of the family; ultimately she was the one with the say on what expenditures were made.

Three-and-a-half weeks later, Iris opened her business with limited stock but unlimited enthusiasm. She hosted stamp parties, had stamping clinics at the shop, and went to local schools and senior centers and held art classes. She was tireless. And it showed. She'd tapped into a steady stream of women and children who liked stamping and wanted to do more of it.

Eban was sure this initial interest would wane. To his surprise—and to Iris's and Helena's delight—demand for stamping remained strong. Iris's business thrived, while Eban's withered. Cost increases for chemicals and insurance were causing him headaches.

Once again, the family met at the dinner table. Only this time the discussion was more awkward. The dry cleaning business that had been their bread and butter was failing. The dry cleaning shortfall each month was being covered by the new stamping business. Helena knew they had to close the dry cleaning business before it sucked all the money from the stamping business. Eban was distraught. "Close the business? I have twenty-five years of my life invested in that business! It would be like cutting off an arm and a leg."

Helena told him: "It's been a good run, Eban. Now it's your daughter's turn. Be happy. Help her be successful."

Eban went into a deep funk. Couldn't eat. Couldn't sleep. Couldn't bear that Helena had told their landlord they wouldn't be renewing the dry cleaning storefront's lease. He thought his business life was over.

It was his daughter who pulled him out of it. Bit by bit, Iris kept asking for his help. Of course he couldn't refuse her; he loved and appreciated his daughter. And before Eban realized it, Iris had him spending the entire workday at the shop—manning the register, unloading inventory, packing shipments, sending out flyers.

Eban, smiling broadly, will now tell you losing that arm and leg was hard, but it was for the best.

+   +   +

Eban's story illustrates two points. The first is that sometimes in a declining business you have to amputate that part of the business that's dragging you down—even if it was your core business and what's left is an offshoot. It takes incredible fortitude. But it's the right thing to do if you're fighting gusty headwinds of market forces.

The second point is about where family members were in the personal life cycle.

Eban, at close to 60, was in preretirement mode. He'd built his business and wanted it to carry him to retirement. His idea of enlarging the shop was wishful thinking that a bigger space would lead to increased income and profit. It allowed him to avoid dealing with why his business was really declining. Had he faced it, he would have realized it was a battle he couldn't win. Business and personal life cycles were conspiring against him.

Iris was in her late 20s, with that I-can-do-anything mentality. A shop that sold rubber stamps probably didn't have the best chance of succeeding, but Iris was oblivious to all the risks and pitfalls. She was a 20-something with a business in its early growth stage. Her energy and enthusiasm were the factors that made her business a success (see Figure 16.1). Although having Helena watching her back and her income and outflow didn't hurt, either.

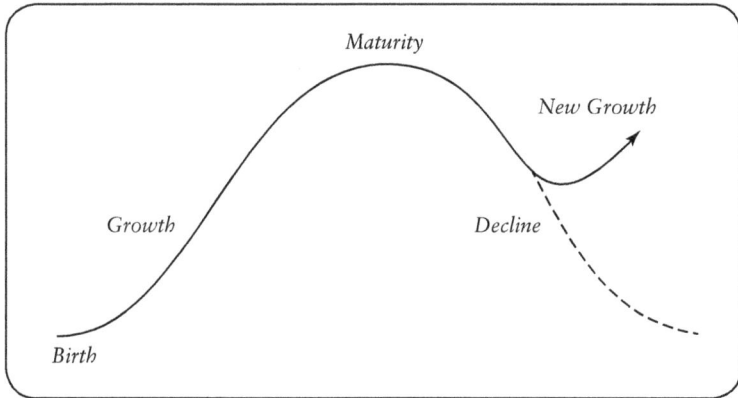

Figure 16.1 Moving from Decline to New Growth

OUT OF SURGERY, INTO RECOVERY

A declining business must do whatever's necessary to return to growth mode. That journey can take many different paths. For Rick and Ben, it was rightsizing the business to fit their new income. For Eban, it was shuttering his business to focus on his daughter's.

Neither had an easy time of it. If you face this situation, you probably won't find it painless, either. What should sustain you is the knowledge that you're surviving; you're on the road to recovery and your business is once again poised to thrive.

Exercises:

☑ What does your company's blood work tell you? What trends do you see? Where is revenue rising, and where is it falling? If you have a revenue stream that is now a revenue trickle, do a PEP analysis on why income is falling.

☑ As much as you don't want to do it, would surgery help your business become fit again? What would you have to cut? What would be the cost? How would it alter your business moving forward?

CHAPTER 17

REBALANCING: REPEAT

If rebalancing is important to a newly growing, formerly mature business, it's even more important to the declining business that's paid a heavy price to return to growth mode.

Obviously aligning your management and support staff to the restructured business is the most crucial area. But before we move on to those, let's not forget all the other areas that need attention—office space, fleet vehicles, and equipment and supplies. Each of these needs to be adjusted to your new reality.

I recently walked through the cube farm of a business that had been forced to cut deep. Of the sixty cubes only seven were occupied, and those seven were scattered all over the space. Walking past those empty cubes was spooky. Depressing, too. No banter. No laughter. No phones ringing. No kids' pictures pinned to the wall. No smells of coffee or food eaten at the cube. Just the sound of emptiness.

For the people left working there it would be a constant reminder of friends gone. Better to move employees together so they're not sitting by themselves and feeling alone.

It's a small thing. But improving morale after a downsizing is actually a big thing. Anything you can do to help, especially early on, will pay big dividends. So attend to the "stuff" part of rebalancing, too.

TEAM REBALANCING

We've talked about rebalancing to resize the organization to match its revenue. We've also talked about weeding out zombies. Both will change the size and complexion of your management team and/or department heads.

This is a rebalancing change you'll need to watch closely. You want good chemistry between key individuals in the organization. How important is that chemistry?

Undoubtedly, you've watched either college or pro basketball. By the time players have reached the college level, they're skilled players. So when a team plays poorly, it's usually not because the players aren't talented. It's because they aren't playing as a team. The chemistry just isn't there. Why not? Here are some obvious scenarios:

- **You have one star player who thinks he's better than the others.** He's only interested in his stats and the other players resent him. Quickly, the game becomes him versus them.

- **You have two members of the team who have played together before.** The two of them have chemistry and want to do things the way they've done them before; they don't want to accept the new system.

- **All five team members are vying to be the team leader.** Not one of them wants to concede anything to the others. This usually results in finger pointing and backbiting. If one does begin to stand out, the others will sabotage him or her.

- **You have a zombie in the group.** The group either feels an obligation to carry that person or resents carrying him or her. Either way, you're playing with four people instead of five.

- **You have five players who are in agreement on one thing**—they don't like your coaching and are bound and determined not to do what you tell them.

Fixing any of these issues is difficult but not impossible. Just as you've seen the teams that play poorly, you've seen teams that excel. They're unselfish. Driven. And joyous. Five individuals seemingly playing as one. (Tons of insightful books by successful coaches have been written on team building. Head to the bookstore or find articles online. It's easy to learn from some of the best in the game.)

My point is that you have a dynamic in your management team that can either pull you forward or push you back. Look at your guys and gals and sort out your situation.

A couple of years ago, I thought I'd built the dream team here at Apollo. I brought in a heavyweight with outside experience that I was confident would invigorate our business. The chemistry with the rest of the team never jelled, however. The heavyweight could neither get along with the team nor with me. I realized my hiring mistake and gave him the boot. His replacement turned out to be a breath of fresh air. About the time he was settling in, another member of the team went zombie on me. Pretty much retired on the job. So I had to deal with that situation and rebalance, yet again.

Don't be afraid to rebalance multiple times a year if you have to. And if there's a zombie in the group, deal with that immediately. Whether your management team feels an obligation or hates that person's guts, that individual is sucking their attention away from what's important—building the business.

Once you're zombie free, do an assessment of the strengths and weaknesses of the remaining team. Do they mesh? Do they complement each other? How well do they get along at work? How well do they get along outside of work?

That last one means you may need to arrange a bonding event outside of business hours. It will give the team time to get to know each other and it gives you an opportunity to evaluate them as a group.

Bonding events can be simple—a happy hour. Or elaborate— a Caribbean cruise. Find something that's comfortable for you, and for them.

I knew a group—four men and two ladies—who went on a whitewater-rafting trip down the lower Gauley River in West Virginia. They spent time talking in the van on the way there, had a heck of a time navigating the rapids, and returned home as good friends who had shared a common adventure.

What did the company get for that investment? I think this management team watches out more for the company and for each other now. Not that they didn't before. But now they're more diligent about it. Things don't fall through the cracks. Opportunities aren't missed. Instead of lackadaisical play, you see a team in sync.

This is what you want. You want everyone in sync and pulling the company forward. To jump back to basketball, you want your team to make a deep run into March Madness.

But like the college game—or the pro game, for that matter—each year is a new year. Guys graduate. Injuries happen. New guys get the opportunity to step up and play. You might say every basketball team rebalances each season.

You should be thinking about rebalancing that same way. Every year you should be reevaluating two things:

- **Do my foundational support services align with the size of the business?** If not, what do you have to do to get the two in alignment? Do you need to cut staff? Do you need to add a support service? Has technology changed how your support staff should function? How long do you expect balance to last? Three months? Six months? A year?

- **Do I have a management team that's playing together and pulling the company forward?** If not, do you need to eliminate, move, or add an individual? What can you do to make them more of a team? How long do you expect balance to last? Three months? Six months? A year?

Don't view rebalancing as a chore. Think of it as optimizing your business, recalibrating it to best meet the challenges you'll face.

Exercises:

☑ When was the last time you rebalanced your support services? How about your management team?

☑ Is your management team working in sync? Or do they operate in silos pretty much doing their own thing? What can you do to bring them together as a group? Have you tried a bonding activity? If you did and you didn't get the results you wanted, try again. One may not have been enough. In my experience, the more bonding, the better.

CHAPTER 18

ZOMBIES DIDN'T EAT MY BUSINESS

They tried. Oh, how they tried.

I'm happy to tell you Apollo has been zombie free for a good three to four years now. That doesn't mean I won't walk into the shop tomorrow morning and find one skulking about the place.

But if I do, I know what to do about it. And if you've been reading closely, you do, too. Let's recap.

ZOMBIE REHAB

No matter what phase the company is in—growth, maturity, or decline—there may be zombies that are important for the company to retain. Often they're people with institutional knowledge, a key customer relationship, or a slice of ownership. These are people you know will be valuable to the company if you can get them back from the undead.

You have to get these people out of their ruts. Try unburdening them of all the tasks they found onerous and slowly begin to involve them in new challenges. I'm referring to these new challenges as "zombie rehab." They're new, different, and may reignite that spark that made these people so valuable to the organization.

ZOMBIE INFESTATION

If you have zombies and the situation has gone untreated for some time, you may have what I call a zombie infestation. It probably started with one zombie and that person infected others. Often this manifests itself in departmental slowdowns, increasing job times, and silo-type behavior.

There are two ways to deal with an infestation. The first is to identify the leader and in no uncertain terms let him know this zombie-like behavior is unacceptable. Don't expect this to do any good. The alpha zombie will defy you. But you've now served notice, and when this person's behavior doesn't change, you put him on a work plan and manage him out of the company.

This person's dismissal may be enough to salvage the others who are infected. You'll need to monitor that situation closely. If you don't see signs of a return to normal, give the group a warning. If this still doesn't work, you have no recourse but to put all of them on a work plan, worst offenders first.

The second way to deal with an infestation is to eliminate the entire nest. Back up what needs to be saved, gather what institutional memory you can, and then give the whole department notice.

Let me reiterate: don't tell them you're letting them go

because they're zombies. Lawsuits. Remember? Let them know you don't think the department is working at the level needed and you'd like to reorganize it with a clean slate.

And, in fact, a clean slate may be what *is* needed. You'll get a faster rebuild and better performance using people who aren't infected to help you rebuild.

SOLO ZOMBIE

Solo zombies can be one of two types. The first is the line worker. I've had techs who have gone zombie. Once productive team members, they have trouble getting their work finished on time, gripe about every little thing, and are hostile about management.

Unfortunately, these are individuals who interact with your customers and can sour those relationships very quickly. My advice is to deal with them quickly and firmly. The damage they can do will take your breath away.

The second type of solo zombie is higher in the organization. They may be mid-level managers or department heads, positions where they can inflict damage on those below them and cause angst for those above them. Often, they can be salvaged by a series of specific performance reviews, but if that fails, find someone worthy and make the replacement.

SLEEPER ZOMBIES

Sleeper zombies, you'll remember, are usually caused by a triggering event: not receiving a promotion. A casual reprimand. Problems at home. Frankly, almost anything—not finding a good parking place that morning—can serve as the trigger. Once that happens, it sets them off and they start doing anything they can to be disruptive.

Because they haven't been infected long, you can often get them to reveal what's really bothering them. Remember, the triggering event was just the tipping point. It's what happened prior to that that's important to learn. Once you do, you can make a call as to whether you can salvage this individual or move on to dismissal.

END-STAGE ZOMBIES

These are those employees in their 50s or 60s who have retired on the job. Let's talk about those closest to retirement first. If you have an employee a year or two from actual retirement, you may want to move that individual to a position where he can't hurt the company as he finishes out his career. Remember, end-stage zombies aren't malicious; they just want to finish out their workdays quietly. Treating them harshly will make you the bad guy. Find a nice corner and have them sit in it.

Younger end-stage zombies are more of a problem. These individuals may be senior in the organization, or even hold a mid-level manager or department head title. They may think they've earned the right to spend the next ten years or so sleeping at their desks.

Don't put up with it. Call them out on it. Challenge them. See if they perk up. If not, it's time for a work plan. Don't hesitate to move them out of the organization if you don't see improvement. If they are a problem at 50, they'll be even worse by 60.

Undoubtedly, there are other types of zombies. But these classifications cover the most troubling. They're also the most troublesome the further along your business happens to be on the growth, maturity, and decline business life-cycle continuum.

Like shoplifters, zombies are a difficult and expensive problem. Smart stores have systems to minimize the impact of shoplifters. I would encourage you to do the same for zombies.

At first sight, deal with them. Don't let them get away with it.

Exercises:

☑ Do you have a zombie or zombies in your organization that you believe are worth saving? Diagnose what's causing the zombie behavior and then put together a treatment plan.

☑ Have you been the victim of a zombie infestation? If so, how long has it been going on? What might your best plan of treatment be? Isolate the alpha zombie and deal with that person? Remove the entire department? Take some other course of action? How will you explain the problem and what you're doing to correct it to the rest of the organization?

☑ Can you identify any solo zombies in your organization? What is your plan of action for dealing with these individuals?

☑ Sleeper zombies are especially difficult to treat. If you spot one, note the triggering event, but work with that individual to discover the issues causing zombie behavior.

☑ Do you have end-stage zombies in their 50s? 60s? How do the two differ? How should your treatment differ?

CHAPTER 19

UPPING YOUR GAME

People are always asking me, *Jamie, why are you so intent on making waves? Why can't you be content with the way things are?* I don't think I'm intent on change for the sake of change. I'm always looking at the business from the perspective of asking: How can I make it better? How can I up my game?

In *Squirrels, Boats and Thoroughbreds*, I talked about living a purposeful life by practicing four-dimensional leadership: leadership in your personal, family, business, and community lives. Personal and family are at the beginning of the order because they're your first priority. But business leadership is where you can make a difference not only for you and your family but also for your employees and their families.

Your business is the foundation that makes that possible. If your business is plateaued or declining, you're not going to be able to thrive, nor will you be able to help your employees thrive. Business growth, resulting from your leadership, is what makes it possible for good things to happen.

If you have a mature traditional business, as I did, and you continue to do what you've always done, you'll have the same results. I wanted more. And the only way to have more—more personally, for my family, for my business, for my community— is to change things for the better. Change, when you look at it that way, hey, it isn't so bad.

In fact, change can do wonderful things. I've concentrated on three of those things that are important to a traditional business:

- Keeping a growing traditional business growing.

- Helping a mature traditional business grow instead of sliding into decline.

- Reversing the fortunes of a declining traditional business and starting it growing again.

All three are worthy challenges. And like any good challenge, it won't be easy or happen quickly. But the good you can do— for yourself, your family, your business, and your community— makes it so important that you step up, commit, and persevere.

In this book, I've tried to give you tools and stories that will help you on your journey. They say: *It's lonely at the top.* I'd add that it's loneliest as you try to institute change. But on the other side of change are satisfactions that are amazingly fulfilling.

Each day when I walk into the office, I'm greeted by a positive vibe of energy. Everyone is pulling the company forward, making the most of each opportunity. It wasn't always that way, and I take satisfaction in knowing I was the catalyst that made it happen.

When I meet with our executive team, I take satisfaction in knowing we've got a talented group that works as a team. I'd match them against any company's management team. I think they're that good.

But perhaps the biggest difference between the Apollo of today and the Apollo of years past is that we made the pilgrimage and drank from the fountain of youth.

Thanks to that magic elixir, this is not an old company any more, stuck in its ways and unwilling to change. This is now a young company that believes it can better deliver core services and that is constantly looking to add new services.

This is a fun place to work. Our customers are entrusting us with more and more of their business. I'm having a blast.

I want that for you, too.

As that happens, as you join me on this journey, I hope you'll share with me how you're transforming your traditional business.

Together we can revitalize our segment of the economy and bring new life to our companies, our families, and Main Street, USA.

Exercises:

☑ What will it take for you to commit to upping your game?

☑ How could your business leadership spark improvements in your personal, family, and community life?

☑ How can you encourage other traditional business CEO/owners to transform their traditional businesses?

CHAPTER 20

THE REST OF THE STORY . . .

One of my pet peeves is that tech companies get all the attention. It's Google this and Apple that. Which is fine, they're great companies and they've added to the business landscape. But let's not forget that the backbone of American business is traditional companies like yours and mine. Yet you hear little—darn little—about us.

The story I'd like to read on the front page of the *Wall Street Journal* or in a glossy spread in *Fortune* or *Businessweek* would go something like this.

The New Business Engine: Traditional Businesses Spark an American Renaissance

Who saw this coming? The best and brightest of our young people are no longer automatically heading to Silicon Valley or Wall Street. Instead, they seem to be flocking to Main Street. And it's causing a surge in the GNP the likes of which the country hasn't seen since the boom following World War II.

The Bureau of Labor and Statistics reported economic growth of 20.5 percent in companies with under a hundred employees. That surge in traditional businesses has lifted the GNP, long stuck in the 0.0–2 percent range, to a high of 6.1 percent.

And Americans are enjoying a good feeling in their pocketbooks according to Dan Kayser, a respected industry economist. "We're experiencing a new era of prosperity. Unlike the 1980s and 1990s, when only the wealthy got wealthier, this economic cycle is benefiting everyone."

Professor of applied sciences Zane Pockrandt agrees. "This isn't an isolated trend. It's a phenomenon that's sweeping the country. Every state, every ethnicity is experiencing this increase in prosperity."

"It's definitely creating a larger, stronger middle class. When you take a look at the statistics, their buying power is up, and their debt is down. This is what America needs," Kayser adds.

Can it last? Will Case, chief economist for the Norwood Institute, thinks so. "Our research shows widespread growth and hiring in the traditional business sector and we're forecasting continued growth well into the future. The numbers are impressive: employment is up 31 percent, revenue by 27 percent."

"These jobs at traditional businesses are good jobs," adds Lauren Hagin, a human resources director. "They pay a good wage, offer benefits and the chance for advancement. People who want to build better lives for themselves are attracted to this kind of an environment. It's good for them and good for the company."

Traditional businesses, those mainstays of the community such as plumbers, small manufacturers, and heating and cooling companies, have done business the same way for years. No longer.

A new breed of CEOs and owners are applying the latest business techniques and transforming these stodgy, sometimes plodding, businesses into exciting places to work. That philosophic change has attracted young people who want to make something happen. These new traditional businesses are designed to allow employees to earn as much and go as far as their talents will take them.

For the 20- or 30-something who doesn't want to slog in the trenches at Google for ten years before gaining an opportunity to make a difference, these traditional businesses allow those individuals to make their mark virtually immediately. MBAs that wouldn't have dreamed of working at a traditional business are, in effect, now saying: "Sorry, Wall Street, I'm headed to Main Street."

And what's good for Main Street is good for America. That GNP of 6.1 percent has our economy flexing its muscles. Traditional businesses, in communities from California to Washington State, Illinois to Louisiana, Maine to Florida, have become the growth engines of our economy.

And boy, are those engines humming.

+   +   +

Is that craziness? I sure don't think so. Traditional businesses have always been a big part of the US economic picture. But in many ways, we're our own worst enemy. The repetitive nature of traditional businesses dooms us to lack of real growth. We do the same things, experience the same results, and resist anything that smacks of change.

But growth *is* change.

We need to embrace that change, not leave the room when the subject comes up.

Just think what would happen if every traditional business in growth mode continued to grow instead of maturing, if every mature traditional business added a service or product and returned to growth, and if every declining traditional business reversed that trend and started growing again.

It would be the renaissance of Main Street.

It's not craziness. It can happen. All it takes are CEOs/ owners—like you and me—to step up and believe we can reinvent ourselves as a force for the better.

So when you finish this book, don't put it on the shelf and forget about it. Make a list of what your traditional business could do to become a growth engine. Add a complementary service. Offer a new product. Whatever it is, don't put it off. Put it on paper and then write a list of the things you need to do to make it a reality.

Remember, accomplishing something big and important always appears daunting at the start. Begin with one thing on your list, and once you've finished that, move on to the next item. As you work your way through your list, those smaller tasks will add up to a big accomplishment.

As more and more of us achieve those big accomplishments, we'll help generate an economic upturn.

And as more and more of us are able to participate in that economic upturn, that new era of prosperity will span the nation.

C'mon, folks, we can do this. Let's make this story a reality.

FOLLOW MY BLOG POSTS

If you enjoyed this book, I invite you to read my earlier book, *Squirrels, Boats, and Thoroughbreds*, and to follow me on my blog at: JamieGerdsen.com.

SPEAKING ENGAGEMENTS

I am available to speak at conferences, conventions, business meetings, and business schools, in the United States or abroad. To inquire as to rates and availability, pleae contact Lori Ames at ThePRFreelancer, Inc.—lori@theprfreelancer.com or 631-539-4558. For more information about me, please visit JamieGerdsen.com.

www.ingramcontent.com/pod-product-compliance
Lightning Source LLC
Chambersburg PA
CBHW031402180326

41458CB00043B/6583/J